Words of Praise for
Life's a Journey—Not a Sprint

✠

"Jennifer Lewis-Hall's story is part autobiographical and all inspirational. It's very readable and packed with advice that is very useful—for the mind and the body."

— **Rodney Brooks,** USA Today

"Jennifer Lewis-Hall's upbeat, informative, and candid advice is thoroughly readable and do-able—whether you're in a rut or on an endless treadmill. This book gives you vital encouragement to stay in the race at your own pace."

— **Patrik Henry Bass,** books editor, *Essence* magazine

"*Life's a Journey—Not a Sprint* is a must read, both for women starting out in their careers, and for everyone else— the neophyte and the veteran on the road of life. It's a book whose story and wisdom transcend age, gender, and race."

— from the Foreword by **Acel Moore,**
Pulitzer Prize–winning columnist for the *Philadelphia Inquirer;* founding member of the National Association of Black Journalists

✠

LIFE'S A JOURNEY—
NOT A SPRINT

Other Hay House Titles
of Related Interest

৵৾৽৾৵

BOOKS

Inner Peace for Busy Women:
Balancing Work, Family, and Your Inner Life,
by Joan Borysenko, Ph.D. (available September 2003)

A Relationship for a Lifetime:
Everything You Need to Know to Create a Love That Lasts,
by Kelly E. Johnson, M.D.

Shape Magazine's SHAPE YOUR LIFE:
4 Weeks to a Better Body—and a Better Life,
by Barbara Harris, Editor-in-Chief, *Shape*® magazine,
with Angela Hynes

Youth Survival Manual:
1,000 Resources to Prepare You for LIFE!,
by Tavis Smiley and Andrea Foggy-Paxton (available October 2003)

AUDIO PROGRAMS

Dr. Phil Getting Real: *Lessons in Life, Marriage, and Family,*
by Dr. Phil McGraw

Financial Freedom: *Creating True Wealth Now,*
by Suze Orman

Tuning In: *Listening to the Voice of Your Soul,*
by Cheryl Richardson

CARD DECKS

Comfort Cards, by Max Lucado

Empowerment Cards, by Tavis Smiley

If Life Is a Game, These Are the Rules,
by Chérie Carter-Scott, Ph.D.

Until Today Cards, by Iyanla Vanzant

Words of Wisdom for Women Who Do Too Much,
by Anne Wilson Schaef

❧❀☙

All of the above are available at your local bookstore,
or may be ordered through Hay House, Inc.:

(800) 654-5126 or (760) 431-7695
(800) 650-5115 (fax) or (760) 431-6948 (fax)
www.hayhouse.com

LIFE'S A JOURNEY— NOT A SPRINT

*Navigating Life's Challenges and Finding
Your Pathway to Success*

Jennifer Lewis-Hall

HAY
HOUSE

Hay House, Inc.
Carlsbad, California • Sydney, Australia
Canada • Hong Kong • United Kingdom

Copyright © 2003 by Jennifer Lewis-Hall

Published and distributed in the United States by: Hay House, Inc., P.O. Box 5100, Carlsbad, CA 92018-5100 • *Phone:* (760) 431-7695 or (800) 654-5126 • *Fax:* (760) 431-6948 or (800) 650-5115 • www.hayhouse.com • *Published and distributed in Australia by:* Hay House Australia Pty Ltd, 18/36 Ralph St., Alexandria NSW 2015 • *Phone:* 612-9669-4299 • *Fax:* 612-9669-4144 • *e-mail:* info@hayhouse.com.au • *Published and Distributed in the United Kingdom by:* Hay House UK, Ltd. • Unit 202, Canalot Studios • 222 Kensal Rd., London W10 5BN • *Phone:* 020-8962-1230 • *Fax:* 020-8962-1239 • *Distributed in Canada by:* Raincoast • 9050 Shaughnessy St., Vancouver, B.C. V6P 6E5 • *Phone:* (604) 323-7100 • *Fax:* (604) 323-2600

Design: Amy Gingery

Library of Congress Cataloging-in-Publication Data

Lewis-Hall, Jennifer
  Life's a journey, not a sprint : navigating life's challenges and finding your pathway to success / Jennifer Lewis-Hall.
    p. cm.
Includes bibliographical references (p.   ).
  ISBN 1-4019-0189-1 (hardcover) — ISBN 1-4019-0190-5 (tradepaper) 1. Success—Psychological aspects. 2. Success in business. 3. Women—Psychology. I. Title.
  BF637.S8L455 2003
    158.1—dc21

                                        2002155853

                  Hardcover ISBN 1-4019-0189-1
                  Tradepaper ISBN 1-4019-0190-5

                  06 05 04 03   4 3 2 1
                  1st printing, May 2003

                      Printed in Canada

To my parents,
Evelyn and Arthur Lewis,
with all my love

Contents

❧⚭❧

Note: All quotes and letters contained in this book are true. However, except for experts, names and identifying details have been changed to protect subjects' privacy.

FOREWORD

by Acel Moore

Jennifer Lewis-Hall's story is a compelling and detailed account of how she has negotiated the curves, hurdles, and bumps on the road to success in the demanding and deadline-intensive profession of broadcast journalism.

And she's had to balance that challenge with those of being a woman, a mother, and a wife. *Life's a Journey—Not a Sprint* is both an autobiography and a guidebook, offering practical dos and don'ts on how to juggle a career with the demands of work and family life. As Jennifer says, "This book is for the millions of women like me who feel challenged wearing any number of hats in their day: mommy, wife, worker, daughter, sister, tutor, college student, Sunday-school teacher, chief operating officer, first-time job seeker . . . and the list goes on."

Hers is a classic account of the particular challenges faced by an African-American woman who's also the mother of two children and the wife of a corporate executive. Jennifer has succeeded in all these roles. She's been a journalist for 20 years—since 1999, she's worked as a national correspondent for CNBC, covering business, finance, and Wall Street—her reports air throughout the business day. She has often filled in as anchor in CNBC's *Business Day* programming as well as on the NBC syndicated programs *Early Today* and *The Wall Street Journal Report*.

Most important, she's happily married to Joseph Hall and is the proud mother of two well-adjusted children. Why the success? The innocent observer might say, "Well, this is a woman with intellect, confidence, and discipline," and that observer would be right. But, as Jennifer asserts emphatically in *Life's a Journey— Not a Sprint,* credit goes also to the support she's received from her family, parents, friends, and mentors.

Jennifer's most important supporters are her parents, Arthur and Evelyn Lewis. Her father has had a stellar career as this country's first African-American special agent in charge of a federal law enforcement agency. Her mother was a homemaker who was the primary caretaker for Jennifer and her two older brothers.

Her parents had an equal but distinct impact on Jennifer's life. They taught her and her brothers to strive for excellence, to value education, and not to fear taking risks. You can see the result: All the Lewis children are professionals with graduate degrees. (Jennifer is a graduate of Douglass College at Rutgers University with a degree in economics and finance. She also earned a master's degree in journalism from the Medill School at Northwestern University in Evanston, Illinois.) Her mother, who delayed her education to raise her children, reentered college after they left the nest and earned her own bachelor of arts degree.

As a proud mentor to Jennifer, I'm not surprised by her success. I first met her more than two decades ago when she was an undergraduate at Rutgers. When she came to me for advice on developing her writing skills, she told me that she wanted to be a broadcast journalist. It was clear then that she knew what she wanted to do, had developed a career road map, and knew where she was on it. Many students I've counseled over the years knew *where* they wanted to go but weren't sure *how* to get there—mainly because they lacked a sense of where they were at the moment. Jennifer always had that sense. She knew she did, but she came to me for confirmation. I ended up writing a reference letter for her to get into graduate school.

In *Life's a Journey—Not a Sprint,* Jennifer offers tips for facing and dispelling the doubts one has when beginning a career. She says, "I took the slow and steady road rather than the fast lane. My hope was that by first learning as much as I could behind the scenes, I would somehow gain a bit of an edge." That approach paid off. She began her career as a print reporter for the *Philadelphia New Observer,* a local weekly newspaper. Then she worked for *Black Enterprise,* a national business magazine in New York. She began her broadcasting career at KYW-TV in Philadelphia as a producer for *Evening Magazine,* a nightly newsmagazine program.

Jennifer also offers advice on keeping your marriage intact and maintaining love and intimacy with your spouse. In defining love, she asserts that you have to take the time to be with yourself in order to love someone else. She emphasizes the importance—in all parts of life—of keeping in good physical shape, and shares her exercise and diet regimen. She even includes recipes for healthy but tasty foods. But the book provides more than just one woman's wisdom—it also offers advice from professionals such as Harvard's Alvin Poussaint, M.D., a nationally recognized psychiatrist specializing in family matters.

Life's a Journey—Not a Sprint is a must-read, both for women starting out in their careers and for everyone else—the neophyte and the veteran on the road of life. It's a book whose story and wisdom transcends age, gender, and race.

Acel Moore is an associate editor, columnist, and member of the editorial board of the *Philadelphia Inquirer*. He is a Pulitzer Prize winner and a Nieman Fellow. Moore, who started as a copy boy at the *Inquirer* in 1962, is a founding member of the National Association of Black Journalists (NABJ). His column, "Urban Perspectives," appears twice a week on the commentary page of the *Inquirer*.

PREFACE

Although I didn't plan it that way, this book has been 20 years in the making. That's just about how long I've been in the television news business, and I've also spent much of that time as a parent and spouse. What I realize now (and strongly believe) is that I was in training, gearing up for managing a very busy household and, at the same time, establishing my dream career as a news reporter.

My life during the past several years reminds me of the growth chart I started when my first son was born. Our precious little one shot up so quickly that in no time at all he surpassed the chart—and his growth spurt has been a barometer of sorts for my family. Our lives just simply took off . . . and what a take-off it was.

After getting married, I worked as a freelance writer during the day and in a department store at night to help offset expenses while my husband worked and attended graduate school for his M.B.A. Then about a year and half later, some really big news came: I was pregnant. Nine months later, I found myself having my husband paged in the library a few times when I thought I was in labor (fortunately, they were false alarms), but I eventually did give birth, and our new addition was the start of something great. Back then, I really had no clue what was in store for me, but now I can see clearly how my life as a mother, wife, and professional has evolved with so much to cherish, yet so many obstacles to move beyond.

So, this book is for the millions of women like me who feel challenged wearing any number of hats in their day: mommy, wife, worker, daughter, sister, tutor, college student, Sunday-school teacher, chief operating officer, first-time job seeker . . . and the list goes on. *Life's a Journey—Not a Sprint* will help you manage your overall life in conjunction with your career as you explore and attain your personal desires. You see, I've spent a lot of time thinking about ways to do things better and about what makes a happier and more rewarding life. I've found, for instance, that it's impressive to have a wonderful job title, but it means nothing if you don't feel that you're personally fulfilled. Consequently, much of my journey has been about being the best I can be at what I do and improving myself on both the inside and out along the way. Acquiring practical tips and techniques to do that has been key.

Many of the tips that I present here and that I hope you'll try come from my own personal experiences in learning to craft a skillful plan for my own success. But I've been fortunate enough to acquire tricks of the trade from informal discussions over the years with my circle of diverse friends and kindred sisters whose backgrounds run the gamut of race, culture, age, and background. Many of them are my sorority sisters, close friends, aunts, and godmothers; others I've worked with professionally or socially in volunteer organizations; some I've met through friends; still others I've been blessed to meet while giving speeches or moderating panel discussions on women's issues.

And so, as I wrote this book, I decided to link my own advice with insights from women across the country who have so much to give. Many of them shared their thoughts with me on their own journey through life and reaching one's potential; some explained how they've used hard times to appreciate life's joys; and others expressed how challenges can become victories in life if we let them. Their heartfelt insights far exceeded my grandest expectations. Like me, many have leaped beyond the seemingly impossible or found ways to recapture parts of their soul that were thought to have been lost forever.

Through this exchange with others, I've become wiser, and as my mother says, "We *all* have words of wisdom and can learn from one another."

ACKNOWLEDGMENTS

Writing *Life's a Journey—Not a Sprint* has been like crafting a quilt into which the many people whom I admire, respect, love, and care about have woven something special.

To my children, thank you for being patient with me. I love you so very much.

To my husband, mother, father, and brothers, I'm grateful for your vision, lending an ear, and always being there for the children.

To my best friends and girlfriends, you're my steady beat of encouragement.

To the entire Hay House staff—especially Reid Tracy, Jill Kramer, Shannon Littrell, Katie Williams, and Stacey Smith—your support and professionalism were amazing.

To my mentors Acel Moore and Kit Melick-Niemiec, I thank you from the bottom of my heart. Individually, thread is plain and simple. But when woven gently, one piece at a time with loving hands, it becomes a beautiful tapestry with vibrant colors. It's in all its glory. You all are those threads for me. Thank you for helping me on this new and exciting journey.

INTRODUCTION

L *ife's a Journey—Not a Sprint* is a guide, a tool for you to use in achieving success within all aspects of your life, including career, family, relationships, and personal well-being. Let it be a way to point you in the right direction to seek a promotion, become a better listener, or find time for yourself.

When I think about my own life, it truly has been a journey and not a sprint. Many people believe that the reporters they see on TV simply arrive there—composed, nicely dressed, and flawlessly made up. Little do they know of the very full existence on the other side of the camera—the hectic mornings getting the kids off to school or running them to the doctor before work. In fact, for me, my days as a newsperson also include plenty of prayer, a lot of faith, and plain old hard work.

I hit many milestones early in my career, despite the naysayers who warned that it would be impossible for me to get very far in this fast-paced, extremely competitive business. With their words in mind, I chose to take the slow and steady road rather than the fast lane. My hope was that by first learning as much as I could behind the scenes, I'd somehow gain a bit of an edge. Usually people race to be in front of the camera; instead, I deliberately did as much writing as I could and even tried my hand at the production end to learn other essential aspects of the field of broadcast journalism.

That strategy isn't very sexy, but it has brought me success in the country's top news markets and in a job that has allowed me to be seen by thousands of viewers around the world. Obviously that path wasn't in the form of a straight line, and needless to say, I've hit quite a few bumps in the road along the way.

Looking back, I call my path the battle between determination and doubt. I was determined to land that first and all-important television job—agents and news directors, however, were more focused on casting doubt on my career goals, discouraging me from trying to break into the business. I knew it wouldn't be easy, and I recognized that I was pretty green. But you see, I was prepared . . . at least mentally. I'd been practicing for my dream since I was in the second grade, using my hairbrush to talk to the "audience," which was really my bedroom mirror. Many times my parents became mock viewers as well.

But no matter how convinced I was that being a TV personality was my true calling, others were skeptical that I'd show up in a major news market or even make it to a network at all. So I set out to defy the nonbelievers. And I've been waging my own little war against them ever since.

Perhaps it's that I'm strong-willed or discovered early on that I'd have to be very persistent. I thank the first agent I ever met for making me more determined than ever to become a television journalist. It was during the late '80s in New York City, and I was fresh out of graduate school. I was thrilled that an agent would even meet with a peon like me. However, things didn't exactly turn out the way I thought they would.

He took one look at me and simply said, point-blank, "You're too fat to be on TV." Then he went on to suggest that I wear only brown lipstick on what he called "big lips."

Obviously this discussion didn't lead to my signing on the dotted line. After that, I realized that I needed a plan if I was going to get my foot in the door of a news station. I thought, *If the odds are* *against me landing something in <u>front</u> of the camera, what about behind the scenes?* So I opened myself up to a range of possibilities.

One position that came along was in producing, a job I really hadn't thought about too seriously. But that's where opportunity knocked, so I answered. I became a studio producer in Philadelphia for a syndicated newsmagazine show in the nation's fourth-largest market. I was one of the youngest people the station had ever hired. Each week, famous models, actors, and sports figures were invited to appear on the show. It was amazing.

Yet I had to learn a lot quickly in a business that at the time still prided itself on people earning their stripes the hard way. It was a trial-by-fire experience, which taught me some valuable lessons I've since passed on to others: (1) Be as prepared as <u>possible</u>. If you truly don't know something, ask someone you can trust. (2) <u>Don</u>'t give up. If you know it's where you belong or what you need to propel you to the next position, hang in there. (3) If the <u>position</u> you want doesn't come your way at first, think about what else you can do within the organization to get you were you're headed.

Fortunately, the career wheels did start turning for me. But to my surprise, my greatest joys and biggest hurdles were yet to come—including marriage, the birth of my children, and the evolution of myself as a woman. Life's events were and still are overwhelming. Wondering how we're going to get everything done and still save a little bit of ourselves for ourselves is something that my friends and I spend countless hours discussing.

I even find myself engaged in similar conversations with people I meet while shopping or traveling. How do you find time for *yourself* in the midst of climbing the corporate ladder and raising kids? Where do you draw your strength from when so many people rely on you? Is there a better way to manage your personal and professional lives to achieve the most out of them? And so, this book is a primer to help you with these issues *and* many more of life's challenges.

Seeking to answer these questions has forced me to look deep inside myself. I encourage you to do that as well. *Life's a Journey— Not a Sprint* will push you to add balance to your life, find out what you're really good at, and relish the things that you enjoy— even when there's very little time to appreciate them.

So I invite you to please join me on a journey that will enrich your life!

PART I

MAKING THE RIGHT CAREER MOVES

CHAPTER ONE

Striving
and
Strategizing

My path has entailed a lot of prayer, careful planning, and perseverance. But there's so much more that I want to share with you regarding my personal life and career, as well as what I've learned from others as I've moved forward each day.

In this book, I'll share my insights on everything from the power of making positive career choices, to living a healthier lifestyle, to thriving within relationships during times when life is extremely challenging. I want you look at your life as a *journey*—one that's developing each and every day and growing despite the bumps along the way.

"I'd tell anyone else who's striving for success to know their strengths and weaknesses—and if they're fortunate enough to be supervisors, they should hire people whose strengths complement those weaknesses."
— Linda, attorney

Let's begin with striving and strategizing, two powerful concepts that women have been involved with for decades, even centuries. Our mothers did it, as did our grandmothers and great-great-grands before them. Just think—most of these women weren't CEOs or M.B.A.'s or Ph.D.'s, but they were very accomplished in something else: their determination to succeed. Sure, I've interacted with many amazing ladies in education, politics, medicine, law, and journalism (my chosen field), but so many of the women who have made a profound impact on my life were those who raised their families and sent their children and grandchildren to private schools and universities even though they'd never gone to college themselves. Allow me to explain what I mean.

The Power of Our Ancestors

Not long ago, I interviewed Maya Angelou about living a full life in a world that's been forever changed since the September 11, 2001, terrorist attacks in New York. The renowned poet and best-selling author said that in looking to the future, we must take heart in remembering our resilience in the past.

> *"We have to realize what we have lived through in America. We have lived through the Revolutionary War; we've lived through slavery. We've lived through the abolishment of slavery; we've lived through the reduction of the Native American tribes. . . . We've lived through the wars—World Wars I and II, and Korea, and Vietnam. We've lived through hate, and we've lived through hope. It's amazing."*
>
> — Maya Angelou

Maya's statement led me to think seriously about the men and women who have made tremendous strides in the world. I realized that my success wasn't a whim or random occurrence—it's been a work in progress. In fact, it started in 1922, when my grandmother, Bianca, a native of the small island of Anguilla in the British West Indies, made her 22-day journey to the United States.

> *"Listening to the success stories from my elders gave me the determination that could be applied in the workplace or in life in general: Get all the education you can (qualify yourself); concentrate in a specific area that best suits your interests; communicate with your peers; be flexible, yet show your strengths; dress to impress; be polite, but don't appear weak; become knowledgeable about different cultures; be respectful; and trust your instincts."*
> — Laura, retired educator

She came with a bagful of dreams stashed away in her homemade cloth suitcase, and the hope of building a future in America. Educated in a one-room schoolhouse on that island, my grandmother had only completed the eighth grade, yet she had an unwavering belief in God, could read and write well, and was trained as a seamstress. This elegant and polished woman also possessed two qualities that I believe many of us need: ingenuity and a tremendous amount of guts. Young Bianca wasn't reluctant to take chances on the things that she truly believed would better her life. And it would be these opportunities—along with exceptionally hard work, her faith, and her confidence in herself—that would shape our family's fabric through the generations.

As she worked in the post office at night and did side jobs such as making and selling flowers, she and her husband (my grandfather), Joel, flourished. They saved their money and eventually purchased several apartment buildings. They educated their children, and after their daughter (my aunt) died as a young mother from cancer, they raised *her* children as well. My grandparents were brave and not afraid to push the envelope.

Taking Chances

What chances are you willing to take on your journey? You see, when you're truly focused and ready to strive for a particular goal, it's time to think about the sacrifices you'd be willing to make in order to get there. You may be seeking a promotion, trying desperately to lose weight, working hard to recapture the zest in your love life, or seeking spiritual nourishment. Regardless of your goal, you must first establish that you're willing to make a change, and then you can become proactive about charting your own path.

In the mid-'90s, I definitely knew I was pushing the limit when I took a job as a general assignment reporter in Philadelphia. The job required me to travel about two hours a day (each way) from my home in New Jersey to the office—and that wasn't factoring in the live-shot locations or stories that would take me to Delaware, various parts of New Jersey, and throughout the state of Pennsylvania. It was a live ten o'clock news show, which meant that I was usually standing in front of a fire, a courthouse, a school, or a murder scene, often filing my story minutes before going on the air.

It may seem crazy to most people that I'd even consider such a rough commute or accept this job when I was a mother with a husband who traveled. But for me, the explanation was easy: I wanted a shot at the network. I even set a timetable as to how long I wanted to stay before moving on to the next level. Yet, as with many things in life, my schedule didn't exactly pan out as anticipated. I'd hoped to leave in about three and a half years—but it actually took about five years to find a better opportunity.

I can laugh now, but I certainly wasn't then. During this stint, I covered every kind of natural disaster—blizzards, snowstorms, floods, power outages, you name it—so I always kept a change of clothes in my car. I had rain and snow gear, boots, hats, and gloves, and so on. In fact, I remember that people had become so familiar with my winter coat that they nicknamed it "the green monster." Yet the value of staying as long as I did was that I was able to use the wealth of these experiences as a stepping-stone, a pit stop that propelled me onto a bigger highway.

This experience gave me a strong work ethic and helped me build my confidence. I knew the job, staff, and territory, and I was clearly ready for, and confident about moving on to the next level.

So weigh the risks and think about the chances you're willing to take in your journey. That next level could be another position that allows for more responsibility, or it could be a move out of the workplace entirely, allowing you to spend more time with your children, go back to school, or help your aging parents.

Asking Yourself Serious Questions

I encourage you to think seriously about what you're passionate about. When it's in your heart, striving to meet your goals becomes much easier than settling for something that you know deep down is second rate.

Don't wait for someone else to ask you the hard questions. The following "career challenge" will help you focus on where you are in your profession and where you'd like to go.

I'd like you to get out paper and a pen, find a quiet place so you can think clearly, and read the following questions and jot down your answers. Don't rush—take your time.

Jennifer's Career Challenge

1. Am I where I want to be at this point in my career, and will my current position lead me to the next level?

2. Do I use the professional relationships in my office effectively?

3. Have I made a list of my accomplishments by writing in a journal each day?

4. Have I connected with people in decision-making positions at appropriate times in and out of the office?

5. Did I find an informal way to gauge how I'm doing with my bosses at least three to six months ahead of my annual review?

6. Have I found a mentor or a person who can review some of my work as well as discuss my strengths and/or shortcomings?

7. Am I volunteering on projects that will boost my visibility or show that I'm a team player?

8. What am I doing to earn the fringe benefits (merit increases, bonuses, stock options, or other compensations) that some select workers receive?

9. Have I made a wish list of all the things I'd love to be doing in this particular office?

10. What is the single most important goal I'd like to accomplish this year?

If you can answer yes to most of these questions, then you're certainly working diligently to move your career forward. Conversely, if you haven't implemented a number of these strategies, now is the time to start.

The goal is to *maximize your opportunities*—use the list to strengthen your weaknesses. For example, if you discover that you've been drifting in your current position for some time, start working on executing the items on the list one by one. Use these techniques to specifically pinpoint areas in which you can make adjustments and improvements on your career path.

Look around your workplace and take note of the path of others in the office. If co-workers with similar experience have moved on, find out what they did to get their promotions. Ask yourself if they were more aggressive when it came time to offer ideas. Perhaps they gained an advantage by learning some of the skills required for the next big promotion on their own time.

Let's go through the list again, this time with some tips that I think you'll find are quite helpful.

Jennifer's Career Challenge and Strategic Tips

1. Am I where I want to be at this point in my career, and will my current position lead me to the next level?

   Tip #1: This helps you analyze whether your current position is something you actually enjoy, and whether it has the value-added duties to move you to the next step. If it doesn't, it's time to seriously consider a change.

2. Do I use the professional relationships in my office effectively?

   Tip #2: If you're using your downtime (or less busy times when work isn't being compromised) to have light-hearted discussions with key players in the office, then that probably means you're getting a feel for what's happening around you. These conversations can lead to valuable tidbits of information (for instance, a manager spoke well of you in the morning meeting).

3. Have I made a list of my accomplishments by writing in a journal each day?

   Tip #3: This is one of my favorites, for it will help keep you organized and on top of the good, the bad, and the ugly that occurs in the office. You can write in your planner about what transpired that day. Did you have a blowup with a co-worker? You can jot that down, as well as thoughts on how to resolve the dispute. More satisfying, however, will be the times you list your accomplishments in different areas. Then when reviews roll around, you'll have a quick and easy way to reference your strong points.

4. Have I connected with people in decision-making positions at appropriate times in and out of the office?

   Tip #4: Not all deals are made between the typical office hours of nine to five. Many professional relationships are built on discussions that occur over dinner or at early-morning breakfast meetings. This means that you should be aware of the way you present yourself at work-related functions outside of the office. Be professional, and don't overdo it when it comes to alcohol. Let the Christmas tree be the only thing that's, well, "lit up" at your company's holiday party.

5. Did I find an informal way to gauge how I'm doing with my bosses at least three to six months ahead of my annual review?

   Tip #5: After a major story, I like to get feedback about how I can improve or perhaps perfect something that needs tweaking. I've found that doing this is a gauge as to how management feels about my performance and whether they think I'm doing a good job. By checking in every now and then well before your review, you'll likely get a sense of how you're doing and, if necessary, you'll have the time on your side to try to make some improvements.

6. Have I found a mentor, or a person who can review some of my work as well as discuss my strengths and/or shortcomings?

   Tip #6: Having a mentor is simply invaluable—it's like having a role model who also has your best interests at heart. (I'll discuss this more in Chapter 4.) There's so much to be said about having someone in your life who can give you constructive criticism, and the support you need to make professional strides. In the end, both parties benefit.

7. Am I volunteering on projects that will boost my visibility or show that I'm a team player?

   Tip #7: You really need to demonstrate that you're capable of working well within a group—few people will consider promoting someone to run a staff or a key position who can't get along with others. So, showcase your talents while proving you can be an important spoke in the wheel.

8. What am I doing to earn fringe benefits (merit increases, bonuses, stock options, or other compensation) that some other select workers may receive?

   Tip #8: This can be a tough one, because there are many reasons why people get company perks. Become involved so that you're on the front lines. This way, your bosses will think of you as someone who's not only doing good work, but an employee who would be missed if you weren't part of the team. This is where you can put your imprint on something special and be remembered for it: It might be a filing system you developed or a list of new clients you've found in an effort to generate new business.

9. Have I made a wish list of all the things I'd love to be doing in this particular office?

Tip #9: This is one of those practical pieces of advice that sounds simple but carries a lot of weight. You need to know what drives you and where the potential opportunities exist within an organization. First, identify the areas that are exciting to you, then you can work on setting your sights on where you want to go and assess why you would be a good candidate.

10. What is the single most important goal I'd like to accomplish this year?

Tip #10: Ask yourself this question over and over to keep yourself focused on why you're working so hard to accomplish a particular aim. Asking the question and knowing the answer will help motivate you, especially on the days when work is frustrating or things aren't going according to plan.

Here's one more tip I've found invaluable: It may seem silly, but don't take water-cooler conversations for granted. If you're going to put your heart and soul into getting ahead, bosses want to know that you're competent. However, they also want to feel comfortable around you.

Be professional, but make people feel at ease when they talk to you. Allow them to see that you can communicate effectively one-on-one *and* in small and large groups. Use the more casual office conversations to chat with your managers about an idea or suggestion you have. Or discuss taking on some added responsibilities. Then, as they say, go for the gold!

Never Stop Striving

Before closing this chapter, I want to show you the first of many remarkable letters from people who shared their journey in work, home, and family with me. This note gets to the heart of why striving for what you want in life personally and professionally is so important.

Dear Jennifer,

I've always been motivated to accomplish whatever I was seeking. If someone told me I couldn't do something, I'd work diligently to prove that person wrong. I remember when I began my career in teaching—my ultimate goal was to become a reading/language arts specialist in my school district. I wanted the position so badly I could taste it. It was a difficult field to enter, but in my heart, I truly wanted to help the students in my district and make a difference.

And so, while raising two very young children, I completed master's degrees in regular education, urban education, and reading/language arts with a management and supervisor's certificate. I finally ended up with an educational specialist degree and am now finishing my doctorate.

Last of all, I am not only a breast-cancer survivor but also a victor. It has been seven years of good health as of September 22, 2002. I am so proud to state that, and so grateful to my Savior and God for leading me through all of this.

Never ever give up. Believe in your cause. God enhances that determination throughout your life if you let Him.

— Sabrina, reading/language arts specialist

As this touching letter clearly illustrates, many people are faced with challenges. Yet they've found the inspiration to keep going by using the positive energy within themselves and generated by those around them to succeed. Again, focus on your dream. Keep it at the forefront of your mind . . . but also close to your heart.

CHAPTER TWO

Finding
Your
Niche

So many of us talk about finding our "niche"—that is, something we're naturally drawn to or really excel at. But the problem is, all we tend to do is talk—we fail to dig deep within ourselves to zoom in on what really gives us the greatest sense of accomplishment or purpose. In this chapter, I'd like to help you find your own particular place in the world.

Learning from the Bumps in the Road

First, I'd like to take a look at how the bumps in life's journey can actually lead to success and help us discover what we're made of.

My mother always says that when I was a little girl, I was set on being really good at something, which Mom suspected would involve either writing, speaking, or both. My brothers, Hunter and Jeffrey, concur, saying that I always loved asking people questions and then telling everyone what they'd said. Somehow reporting seemed to be a natural fit.

I actually got my first big break as a writer when I was in elementary school. My dad was running for the school board, and I wrote his first "official" campaign letter, explaining why I thought he'd be a great candidate. In my letter, which we passed out at shopping malls, I simply stated that he was a great dad and he cared a lot about me. I said that he'd work just as hard to help improve our schools. He won . . . although I really can't take much credit for that.

Then there was the third-grade Christmas play I narrated. Around my neck I wore a huge, uncomfortable star made out of poster board laden with silver glitter. There was so much glitter on it that it practically gagged me throughout the entire performance, and what didn't choke me got in my eyes and scratched my arms. (I guess that's when I found out that being a star isn't necessarily all it's chalked up to be.)

I took part in choir, dance, and plays, but there was a high school essay contest I participated in that my family remembers to this day. The topic was "What's Right about America?" Well, there's a lot right about America—I certainly know that now. But at the time, I couldn't see too much of anything being "right." You see, I was a freshman in high school, and I had to read my essay wearing a red, white, and blue outfit with knee socks and a scarf around my neck. I looked like Uncle Sam in hot pants. (To soothe my nerves, my friends had advised me to look at the people in the audience and envision them in their underwear. I guess it worked, since I won first place.)

My point in sharing those stories with you is that I think it's important to occasionally reflect on the events that have challenged us, for it allows us to remember what it feels like to compete and win (or even come in second place) and have no regrets, because we truly gave that track race or swimming meet our best effort.

Adults tend to tuck away those childhood experiences, pushing them back into the recesses of our minds. However, it can be very healthy to think about them, because they've allowed us to grow and were our first attempts to discover what we're really good at. I realize now that the piano lessons, jazz-dance classes, and singing lessons I took as a kid were really beneficial, and my parents must have understood that. I don't think they necessarily thought that these experiences would propel me to a career on Broadway, but they knew that they'd give me a sense of confidence, which would help me handle many of the challenges the future would bring.

> *"Start with small goals. Challenge yourself. Don't care about the outcome—just do it!"*
> — Jordan, aspiring dancer

Getting the Right Fit

We need to pay more attention to what really moves us in life. That's how I discovered that I was passionate about journalism and would most likely succeed if I chose it as a career. I was always a people person, wanting to know more about individuals and their stories. While many find it nerve-racking, after my "Uncle Sam" speech in high school, I realized that I felt comfortable speaking in front of an audience. And despite the intense competition involved in breaking into journalism, I always believed in my soul that it was the right career for me.

Clearly, I'd found my niche, but I needed to execute my plan. I knew it wasn't going to be easy. People were always warning me that TV news is a business with too many hopefuls and far too few jobs. And I had another issue hanging over my head: I wasn't a likely candidate because of my educational background. Back then, TV newspeople generally had communications or journalism degrees. Who in the world would major in economics (and minor in finance) and think that they were going to be an on-air reporter? Well . . . me.

I believed that journalists could have a background in any field—they just had to have a thirst for writing and a desire to tell compelling stories. They were people who wanted to make a difference in the world using words and pictures. Meanwhile, economics simply seemed like a safe bet. I could handle the numbers and the theory; plus, I'd fallen prey to the philosophy that parents instill in their children that they need to have "something (a secure profession) to fall back on." That's very funny to me now because I can't imagine myself actually teaching economics or being an economist—although I love writing about the economy and how it affects consumers and the broader marketplace around the world.

My experience shows that we should have faith in the decisions we make in life, for they're all a part of our journey. In this instance, it seemed unconventional to many people or even baffling that I wanted to study economics and finance. Was it a mistake? Not at all. Going that route was the best choice for me, as it showed news organizations that I could move freely between various disciplines.

As an undergraduate at Rutgers University, I kept plugging away at supply and demand. I used semester breaks to hustle over to the local affiliate to do internships in television. Yes, I picked up plenty of coffee, sandwiches, and newspapers for the anchors—but I also made an impression and later got a job there. In addition, if there was a chance to write, I'd jump at it. I got my first freelance job with the *Philadelphia New Observer,* a small paper. But this assignment was a plum one—eight days shy of my 21st birthday, I was assigned to cover the International Women's Conference in Nairobi, Kenya.

It turned out that a large delegation of Philadelphia women who were in politics, business, and education was flying to Africa. (Since I often traveled with my mother, I decided to share this once-in-a-lifetime experience with her.) Women from all over the world converged on Kenya to discuss ways of empowering other women, from education to health initiatives. I was responsible for a two-part cover story, featuring topics such as apartheid and a visit to a Masai tribe.

My mother preserved copies of the article in plastic and had them mounted and framed. They're yellow and fragile now, but that doesn't matter. I cherish these mementos.

Here's an excerpt from that first important assignment:

Shillings, pounds, and dollars were all a small price to pay for some 50 delegates who traveled with the Mayor's Commission for Women this July to the largest international women's conference in history. . . . The meeting of the minds from opposite ends of the globe sizzled as the women from Cape Town expressed their grief over the loss of friends, their pain from being separated from their family, and their hatred of the South African laws that had uprooted them from their homes to patrolled campsites, thus eliminating the chance for a normal life.

This experience convinced me that words really could set some positive changes in motion for women living in poverty. And so, I was hooked—I became a real news junkie. I decided to really commit to my niche and do whatever I could to make a career in broadcast journalism happen.

Before I graduated from college, I set out to meet as many people as possible in the field, especially on the television side of the business. I spent time with veteran reporters, producers, and columnists from major newspapers. I asked for pointers on getting started, whether I could shadow them sometime at work, and if it would be okay if I kept in touch.

I set my sights on a master's degree from Northwestern University's Medill School of Journalism. As I waited to hear if I'd be accepted, I interviewed for all sorts of different jobs. I even went to a recruiting session with the Central Intelligence Agency (CIA). The job sounded somewhat exciting, especially since my father had enjoyed an esteemed career in law enforcement. But I was smitten with the idea of becoming a journalist.

Thankfully, I was accepted to Medill, and I was soon packing my bags and heading to Evanston, Illinois. From there, I was off to the nation's capital, Washington, D.C., for the internship portion of my graduate studies.

In D.C., I was a stringer, or freelance reporter, for two media outlets—a television station in Biloxi, Mississippi; and a radio station in Big Pine Key, Florida, which had a population of 5,000. In both cases, my job was to do stories about legislation affecting those areas and get related interviews with senators and members of Congress in those states.

This internship was just one part of my journey. I now had some experience in my chosen profession, but I still had to overcome the hurdle of actually getting into television. As I'd come to find out, that process would surely test whether I'd be steadfast in my belief that I'd found my niche. Would I be willing to stick with it through thick and thin?

I can remember staying up into the wee hours of the morning writing cover letters on my old electric typewriter. During the day, I'd make phone calls to try to get through to news directors. I heard many a "No thanks. We're not interested." But as I tell people that I speak to today, all it takes is one yes. Sure enough, piles of rejection letters later, I finally got a call from an executive at a station in Philadelphia who was looking for a studio producer. It wasn't reporting on-air, but it *was* a job in a major television market (and I'd be getting a salary to boot). To me, it was a golden opportunity.

Still, this was no time to throw a party. After several weeks on the job, I met many people who were glad to see me get my foot in the door. But I vividly remember the day that a key player at the station told me that despite my best efforts, I had three strikes against me: "You're young, black, and a woman."

Of course, his words stung, but I wasn't about to let anyone deter me from my niche. My advice is: Whatever your race, gender, or religion, don't ever let others limit the potential you know exists within you.

> *"Sometimes you just have to go with what makes you feel good. You have to keep trying different things until you find what makes you happy. If you focus on those things that give you joy, then your niche will find you."*
> — Renee, college administrator

Finding your career niche can be an evolutionary process. Yes, I discovered mine early in life and really stayed true to it. But I have a number of friends who've recently found theirs in a profession totally different from the one they've been in for decades. One friend left banking for education; others have said good-bye to successful careers in sales and education, with some choosing to work from home or care for their young children full time.

I find that as we grow, we develop interests in areas other than the ones that enthralled us when we were younger. For instance, these days I find pleasure in fitness-oriented activities, traveling, and gardening. And sometimes interest springs from necessity. I didn't begin gardening until I had a yard that needed a lot of work. After my husband and I purchased a new home, we were looking forward to getting it in order, fixing up everything from overgrown bushes to aging shrubs. At first, the chores were back-aching, and we considered getting a landscaper. In the end, we had a reality check, realizing that we were working with something we'd become very familiar with: a budget.

So I started picking weeds and buying hundreds of flowers that I'd load into the back of the car to plant in the garden. The project led to my buying pots and fertilizer and learning how to care for all different types of plants; I also started to water my garden every day after I got home from work. I soon discovered that what had started out as a chore had become a treasure. I'm certainly no expert, but my little gardening hobby has been a wonderful way to spend some time outdoors and be surrounded by its beauty.

> *"In an attempt to find my niche, I do what makes my heart sing and what might allow others to hear my music."*
> — Jacqueline, artist

Discover Your Comfort Zone

A big part of finding that "life niche" means forcing yourself to ease into it so that you can unwind. Many of us are so busy commuting and rushing to community meetings and sporting events for our children that we never give ourselves a "time out" to relax. Here are ten tips that can help.

10 Tips for Discovering Your Comfort Zone

1. **Think about revisiting some of the things you've longed to do since your childhood** but perhaps put off because of your schooling, job, or family responsibilities. Why not ride your bike or enjoy a freshly scooped ice-cream cone after dinner?

2. **Take time away from your daily routine,** even if it's 15 minutes at the end of the day to think about what comes easily to you and gives you pleasure. Integrate those pleasures—whether reading, writing, or gardening—into your life.

3. **Recognize that finding your niche can be both professional and personal.** If you like arts and crafts but also long to meet new friends, try organizing a craft club. In the workplace, use both your intellectual *and* creative abilities. If you have a knack for both art and computers, perhaps you should pursue graphic design.

4. **Think outside of the box.** Don't see yourself as just one-dimensional, or a "lawyer," a "teacher," or a "school-bus driver." Realize that you're more marketable when you combine your professional knowledge with real-life experiences. For example, if you're a teacher and a musician, integrate those talents into your classroom curriculum.

5. **Know that you have options.** Finding a niche allows for a sense of peace and tranquility in life, but it isn't etched in stone. Our desires ebb and flow, mirroring life itself.

6. **Don't be afraid to try new things!** Your niche may lie in something you've yet to do. If a more advanced position catches your eye, follow through on that pursuit. If you've been eager to take a cooking class, register for one at your local community college.

7. **If your niche isn't healthy, retire it.** Free yourself from bad habits and behaviors.

8. **Make a commitment to take care of yourself,** and find comfort in that. Your niche won't do you any good if you're too burnt out to enjoy it.

9. **Celebrate who you are and what you've accomplished.** It will feel good to give yourself some well-earned credit. Be aware of your achievements, and praise yourself.

10. **Take the helm.** Be the captain of your own ship: Make changes that feel right and fit *your* lifestyle. After all, what's comfortable for someone else may not be for you.

With just a little time and effort, you'll be sure to discover that there's a place in the world that's tailor-made just for you and your talents and interests. Go for it!

☺☺☺☺☺

CHAPTER THREE

Cashing In
on Your
Best Assets

W hen I was a child, my mom and dad used to say, "Everybody's good at something. God gives you talents, so use them."

I truly believe that my parents were right, but the problem is that few of us recognize what our talents are—we underestimate ourselves when it comes to the things we do well. Our gifts can become wasted if we don't capitalize on them, but if they're used, they can advance our careers and enhance our lives. This chapter is about honing in on those talents and utilizing them in order to maximize success.

> *"Take time to search within yourself and assess what you like, what you want to do, and what you're good at. This will change over time—accept it, don't be afraid of it. Remember the bottom line: People want to hire the best folks. You can't just be enthusiastic; you have to be enthusiastic and good. Invest in developing yourself."*
> — Patricia, staffing specialist

Limitless Success

Many people may not think that it's a big deal to get along well with their peers, be respected, and build a cohesive group in the workplace. Yet people with these strengths should consider that they might make ideal team leaders.

Think about the how you can make yourself a valuable asset where you work. Maybe you could start learning various skills that will allow you to flow from one task to another. Or you could begin to prepare for a promotion by getting special certification or taking advanced computer courses. Also, don't underestimate the value of being able to form alliances in the office between groups that have traditionally suffered from a lack of connection. Managers appreciate this skill, and employees who utilize it are often first in line for promotions.

Ask yourself if you're the type of person who can quickly cut through red tape. Do you help your supervisor meet her deadlines?

"Success in the workplace comes down to the following:

1. *Establish good lines of communication with your co-workers and boss.*
2. *Practice positive confrontation.*
3. *Don't take things personally.*
4. *Take responsibility.*
5. *Be heard.*
6. *Know office protocol.*
7. *Be positive; don't commiserate.*
8. *Do excellent work.*
9. *Be on time.*
10. *Go above and beyond when you know it can help.*
11. *And most important—challenge yourself."*
    — Kendra, copy editor

If she's out of the office, can she count on you to fill in where needed and keep the office running smoothly? If so, then you're making yourself a valuable commodity on the job.

The goal is to have what I call *limitless success*—to release any boundaries you've set for yourself that are stifling your goals. It's so easy to think, *I don't have enough time to learn something new,* or *I'm probably not the type of person those managers are looking for,* but you've got to be careful not to mentally remove yourself from a new enterprise for fear of failure.

> *"To have success in the workplace, make a concerted effort to understand the nature of your environment. Develop positive relationships within your company, but also express your ideas with conviction, even if they go against the general consensus."*
> — Janet, Wall Street broker

A big part of limitless success is believing that you *can* put your best foot forward and then proving it. But visualizing yourself in a position and truly embracing the idea of it can be a challenge.

Jeffrey Kahn, M.D., a New York psychiatrist and president of WorkPsych Associates, says, "Most people unwittingly limit themselves. They don't know they're doing it, but the end result can be that they're not as successful as they'd like to be."

Kahn recommends speaking to someone on the job whose opinion you value and whom you think you can trust. Ask them, "Do you think I'm underachieving?" and then look to people who know you well to see if they believe this is the case. Kahn says that what you hear may be a surprise, but other people may see things that you can't objectively see in yourself.

When it comes to climbing the corporate ladder, Kahn believes that people shouldn't underestimate the value of a low-key approach—getting along with people, productive work habits, and personal integrity—for that's a secret route to being successful. He says, "It's better to be confidently assertive rather than angrily aggressive. Productivity is also key." In addition, "Office politics and bureaucracy can be time-consuming, [but you should] focus on what's needed to get the job done. [However], you want to be careful that you're not so super-efficient that you're burning yourself out." He adds that people have to find a balance that focuses on productivity *and* good relationships. Above all, you have to believe in yourself.

What should you do when there's a monkey wrench thrown into your plans? Don't let it put a roadblock on your journey. The following letter perfectly illustrates what I mean.

Dear Jennifer,

When given lemons, make lemonade.

I am a 59-year-old married veteran educator. After 29 years of being a classroom teacher, I served as an administrator in my school district's central office for three and a half years. I liked my friends and colleagues and thought that I had finally "arrived." However, my status changed when my immediate supervisor informed me that my position had been cut from her budget. She told me that I'd be given an opportunity to select a mathematics-teacher vacancy for the next school year or I could retire. My ego was shattered, but I decided that I needed to review the situation in-depth. If I were to choose retirement at age 58, I would have had to take a 6-percent penalty and I wouldn't have been eligible for a new pension-rate change. With this in mind, I chose to teach.

My transition from the central administration office was smooth. Of course, my salary was substantially lower, but I was able to supplement it with a few extracurricular opportunities within the school. As an administrator, I worked for the "company store"; as a teacher, I worked from 7:50 A.M. to 2:54 P.M. with opportunities to be compensated for a variety of duties. For example, I was an academic tutor for students three days a week and a mentor for a new teacher.

Yes, someone gave me lemons that I didn't want, but I found a way to make lemonade. And this lemonade was sweet, because I was able to supplement my salary, utilize my professional talents, expand my professional knowledge, and learn a great deal about the hip-hop world in which we live today. My students really educated me, introducing me to literature, TV stations, videos, and attire. I guess I could have said that sometimes we look at a glass as half empty when it's really half full—I'll always think of it as a glass with lemonade in it.

— Bonnie, high school teacher

"I recently was alerted to the fact that I needed to make a job change. I was comfortable where I was, but I knew I had to branch out if I was going to continue to push myself. In life, some people enjoy staying in a comfort zone, but I personally find that to be unchallenging. And I don't think you can possibly be happy with that mind-set in the long term.

"Many people told me that I was insane for leaving my job without another one to fall back on right away. But I knew I had to pray and take a leap of faith. Three days later, I landed another job—one I actually don't mind waking up and going to in the morning. This experience has boosted my confidence level tremendously. I learned that the best way to attack a problem is to actually attack it—just thinking about it and not <u>actually</u> doing anything about it is not the answer."

— Leah, scriptwriter

What a wonderful example of using your talents *and* changing your thinking when it comes to getting through a complicated situation! When Bonnie and Leah made their transitions, the situations became those they could live with—and they even derived a great amount of satisfaction from them. Their efforts are to be applauded.

Thriving in a Competitive Job Market

If you've recently found yourself back in the job market after a layoff or having children, it can be especially challenging to remember what your professional talents are. But this is the time when it's vitally important for you to focus on your assets so you can confidently nab the position you want.

Peri Hansen is a job-search consultant at Korn/Ferry International, an executive recruiting firm based in Los Angeles. She places candidates into top-level positions. I asked her some pointed questions about the job market and what it takes to shine in the workplace today.

Jennifer Lewis-Hall (JLH): What's the first thing someone looking for a job should do?

Peri: The first thing she should do is assess her strengths and weaknesses. She should write down a list of what she's been able to contribute in the last ten years and what type of legacy she's left behind in an organization. She should then think about how that's applicable to another business or industry. Next, she should ask potential employers what they think of her background and what she can do to gain more experience.

If this person is transitioning into a different field, she should talk to others who have successfully done so. She could hit the college and graduate-school alumni networks, for many colleges have information for people interested in mentoring someone from their alma mater. They see it as a way of giving back something positive to the school. Recognize that people who are working tend to be busy, so ask them if it's easier to communicate briefly over the phone or via e-mail.

JLH: What kind of preparation is needed for those looking for employment? Does a healthy attitude factor into that preparation?

Peri: Of course. However, being positive can be challenging, since a lot of people's self-worth is tied to what they do at the office every day. Being out of work can be a confidence shaker, so they should seek advice and support from friends and family. Job seekers have to stay strong but also continue to project confidence. I tell clients that they also need to be patient and willing to invest time and resources in their search and treat it like a full-time job.

JLH: What are the biggest areas of growth in terms of the job market these days? There had been so much talk about the technology sector as an area of growth and opportunity for job seekers in the 1990s.

Peri: I spend most of my time in the consumer sector, so I suggest that we look at the stock market as a guide: Technology was hit first, especially with so many dot-com companies going from boom to bust.

There have been hurdles across the board for all industries, but strong general-management skills are still in demand. Companies still want salespeople to market their products. And it's great for job seekers to have skills that are "transferable" or can be used in more than one industry.

JLH: How is the job market today different from the years where unemployment was lower and the stock market was racing along?

Peri: Of course it's much more competitive now. Fewer positions are available, and it's more difficult for candidates to find those opportunities. But I don't think it means that there aren't good opportunities out there. Companies still want seasoned talent. They want to make sure that they're making the right choices, because corporations are selective and discerning in hard times. They'll examine a number of qualities that candidates can bring to the table in the future: Can they help the company in the long term with its goals, succession plans, and the training and development of a team? Can they groom others?

JLH: How can a candidate set herself apart from the rest?

Peri: She should learn how to market herself, especially if she's used to coming across internal opportunities and is now looking outside of her company for a job. She should also reach out for help from mentors to assess her strengths and weakness and find a network of industry experts to guide and help her. I'd encourage her to look to former classmates, people she met as an undergraduate and/or in graduate school. They're the people she'd probably feel most comfortable reaching out to.

This individual should think about building that network for the long term, so when she makes her next move, she'll already have a list of contacts to turn to. She can also dip into that network even when things are running smoothly—that is, if she's happy where she is but wants advice about career development.

Peri also advises clients to do the following:

- Think beyond the paycheck. What can this job do to enhance you professionally and personally?

- If you're a stay-at-home parent heading back into the workforce or a first-time job seeker, craft a concise and thoughtful résumé. If you don't have a lot of experience, be honest about that and detail the experience that you do have.

- Talk about the "relationship building" you've done (such as if you've worked with a staff or directly reported to a managing director or school superintendent).

- Carefully proofread your résumé and cover letter; then send them in, along with the note that you'll follow up with a phone call.

- Cultivate a list of contacts, from summer jobs to internships and full-time positions.

- Search Internet job postings.

- Set your expectations accordingly—believe that a job will come, but it may not happen overnight.

- Relax. Re-explore a hobby you haven't had a chance to indulge in.

If you coach Little League, like to exercise in the mornings, or enjoy going to Saturday matinees, continue to engage in activities while your job hunt is under way. Keep in mind that you need to maintain a balance and that mental fitness is a big part of it. In addition, potential employers want to see that you're upbeat and enthusiastic as well as on the ball—not pessimistic and stressed out from your search for employment.

"If you examine the approach of people who have experienced some level of success, you'll find that the majority of them started with a vision. It's within all of us to react to our needs, wants, values, and dreams—a vision provides a compass to help us get to a goal worth achieving.

"To develop a vision effectively, you must fully examine yourself. Determine what you like and don't like, as well as what your values and priorities are. Some people may find that this is an easy thing to do; others may find it to be a long, arduous process that takes years. In either circumstance, it's well worth the effort to develop an internal compass and chart to assist in focusing your career.

"An added benefit of creating an individual vision is that it can help you make appropriate decisions over time as well as select good alternatives that will help avoid or soften pitfalls. A vision can help strengthen you against accepting an alluring possibility that doesn't fit with your plan. Finally, building a dedicated vision will improve your chances of success, as you'll be paying attention to things that you have faith in and that play a significant part in your life."

— Daisy, diversity trainer

If you just take the time to discover the talents that God gave you, you'll be well on your way to a successful journey—in the workplace and beyond.

CHAPTER FOUR

Making the Grade: A Discussion with College Women on Career Opportunities

L ooking back over the past two decades since I graduated, I can really appreciate the profound effect that my college experiences have had on my journey. That's one reason why I felt so compelled to go back and speak with future graduates of my alma mater, Douglass College (an all-women's college at Rutgers University in New Jersey), for an intimate discussion about moving from one's college years toward a career.

> *"I find that women in their 20s confront a major challenge in having to build confidence in themselves and in their abilities, because they're busy trying to find out who they are and where they belong. I find confidence-building extremely challenging, so when my body 'alerts' me to the fact that I'm stuck in a comfort zone or not making any personal progress, I listen."*
>
> — Cynthia, producer

These are the years that really shape our lives, for in college we begin to define who we are and what we believe. We start to see the world through different sets of eyes. And for many of us, it's also when we start to make serious decisions about the path our adult lives will take.

My first day of college set the tone for the next four years: It was both fun and hard work. It was fun because I met my best friend that day, and hard work because we helped our dads move our things up to the top floor of the dormitory (which is where the freshmen mysteriously ended up). This meant climbing about ten flights of steps.

My friend and I had a lot of stuff, and both of our fathers were sweating bullets trying to haul each and every bit. Trunks, televisions, lamps, posters—you name it, we had it. Our parents hit it off that day, and we've been friends ever since.

Those four years at Douglass were indeed fun *and* hard work, but they gave me a wonderful cushion that allowed me to grow before entering the "real world." I certainly saw it as an opportunity—a time to make my own decisions but still lean on others for guidance. I learned things not just by reading them but by doing them. I, like so many other people, went to college to broaden my scope, to see what was out there besides the world I grew up in. So even though I was an economics major, I took courses in theater, jazz, and women's studies. I even accepted a part-time position in the neighboring college's agricultural department for a while just to see what the students studied. This gave me a window into another discipline, and I found out a thing or two about specially bred plants and cultivating prize-winning vegetables.

As it turns out, all the little things I did in college, including working as a resident advisor and being active on campus, were important steps on my journey. I got to know a lot about people from all over the country and other parts of the world; consequently, college made my transition into the working world a relatively pain-free one.

I began to wonder if that process has gotten easier for college students as time has gone on. I inquired about it over a pizza dinner with a group of young women (and Assistant Dean Marjorie White), whom I recently met with at Douglass.

JLH: When I was graduating, I had mixed emotions. On the one hand, I wanted to move on, while on the other, I was very nervous knowing that there would be so many changes. How do you feel about making the transition from college to career?

Tori (senior majoring in public health): Graduating is one big, scary process. Part of me is really ready to go out there and try to make my mark and get involved in what I love. But then there's another part of me that says: "What if I can't find a job? What if I have to go back home and live with my parents?" It's just very scary right now. I'm talking to all the people I've met in order to network. I'm also trying to put together the best résumé that I can, looking at fellowships—using every option.

Sanjana (senior majoring in psychology and women's studies): I'm scared out of my wits. But I'm contemplating graduate school as well as jobs I might want to fall back on. It's certainly an option to work in an area that's not specifically in my major.

JLH: What are you doing to get yourself ready?

Vanessa (senior majoring in communication): I've starting to talk to a lot of people in the workforce. I was surprised, because there's a lot out there that I really wasn't prepared for, even though I'd had many discussions with my mother about corporate America. Entering the job market can definitely throw you for a loop if you don't have anybody to talk to about it. It can be an emotional roller coaster.

JLH: Dean White, can you elaborate on specific things that students can do to become better prepared?

Dean White: Some of the preparation is formal, such as going to career services to address issues of uncertainty (such as what happens if you don't get a job), and most important, to find out how to write a résumé. I can't tell you what terrible résumés I've seen—ones with basic errors such as misspelling. At career services, a pro will look your résumé over for you. If you already have a job, get your boss to look at it. Ask the reviewer, "Based on what I've shown you, would you hire me?" Also, be open-minded about the opportunities before turning down a position.

JLH: But sometimes landing that position entails being prepared _and_ being at the right place at the right time, right?

Dean White: Well, yes. It's very often the case that the position a person acquires is through happenstance. I'm sure you're familiar with the phrase "Luck is when opportunity meets preparedness." To a certain extent, that's true. So, get that application filled out for the professional organization. Seize chances while you're still a student. You may be invited to events in which you're with a lot of professionals—working people, donors, or dignitaries. You have an opportunity to meet people, so don't hover in the corner and miss it. You'd be surprised how many people will give you business cards.

JLH: I did my postgraduate work at Northwestern University— I really knew I wanted to go to graduate school. Do many of you think now that postgraduate studies are the way to go, perhaps to enrich you academically and give you an edge in the workplace?

Fawn (junior majoring in political science and criminal justice): I want to continue my education because I've always been passionate about learning. I really love to learn, and I find it gratifying to be able to help others learn, too. My sister is a high school teacher, and she says it's really important to give back to people. If you can teach one person, it means so much.

You have to be passionate about the things you believe are right for you and will help move you ahead in school and after you graduate. Don't underestimate your skills, and don't necessarily take the first thing that comes along. But my favorite academic advisor gave me some advice that her now-deceased father passed on to her about waiting too long for that perfect job offer. She told me that he'd say, "I understand people are finding themselves; however, there's no good reason they can't work while they're doing it." So essentially, there's a lot to be said about taking a position and recognizing that it's far from being the last job you'll ever have.

The Importance of Finding a Mentor

I'd like to take a break here to talk about mentors and how priceless they can be on your journey. I found mine, Katherine "Kit" Melick-Niemiec, 20 years ago—actually, she found me. At the time, I wasn't looking for a role model, although there were plenty of people I admired. Little did I know that I was about to meet my wise and trusted counselor, a person who would offer advice through my senior year in college and far beyond.

This is an example of why we need to be "open to grace" or receptive to possibilities that can change our lives for the better. You see, I'd been a resident advisor for two years and was asked by the dean to speak at an alumni event on student life. More specifically, she wanted me to discuss my involvement in various activities and programs such as those related to sorority life, student government, and volunteering. I was just weeks away from graduation, and to be honest, my mind was more focused on finals than doing a speech on student life. But I agreed. And, boy, am I ever glad that I did!

At first, I was really nervous about the idea of having to speak in front of the various deans and esteemed alumni, some of whom had graduated decades before me. But I recognized that this was a golden opportunity.

I rushed to put something together, then I decided to speak from the heart and just talk about what I liked to do and why it worked well for me. After I finished, Kit, a soft-spoken, elegant woman who was a newspaper executive and graduate of the class of 1944, came up and congratulated me on my speech. I thought that her doing so was certainly nice enough, but then she really surprised me by telling me how impressed she was and asking if I'd like to visit her office and have lunch. Wow! Could my life get any better at that moment—a free lunch *and* a trip to Manhattan!

So that one brief speech led to a wonderful meeting with the person who would become my mentor and be instrumental in helping me land my first big job. Yes, you need to have the qualifications and take the tests and do the interviews—but it certainly helps to know someone who can advise you on the best way to prepare for the interview process, who can be a reference, and who can provide support by just being a sounding board for your ideas. They're the people who take an interest in you because they see that you're motivated and have a deep desire to succeed.

I don't know how different my career path would have been if I hadn't met Kit that day. It's amazing how things work in your favor when you make yourself stand out in a positive, sincere way. I like to see people at any age have mentors, because they provide such a sense of security and help boost confidence levels—even seasoned professionals need that. And mentors can give you a little nudge in the right direction if and when you get off track.

When I found out that I'd be among a group of extremely distinguished women to be inducted into the Douglass Society, the college's highest honor for those who have distinguished themselves as leaders in their respective fields, I dedicated the speech to my mentor, Kit. Here it is.

A Tribute to Mentors (April 10, 2002)

When I found out I was going to be inducted into the Douglass Society, I couldn't believe it. That's because we sometimes don't see ourselves exactly the way that others see us. We, of course, know that Douglass College women are intelligent, outgoing, capable, and forward thinking. But they are something else: They are women who help other women achieve their goals—even sometimes before we know *exactly* what those goals are.

You see, 17 years ago, in my senior year, a graduate from the class of 1944, Kit Melick-Niemiec, heard me speak in this very same college center, which—not to date myself—was much smaller than it is now. My mentor, whom I just saw two weeks ago, invited me to lunch for the first time in 1985. To make a long story short, she heard of my interest in journalism and from there, as they say, the rest is history. She helped lead me down the right path to a career that I had dreamed of since I was a child.

To women like her who help to shape the lives of so many, I salute you. And what is also key here today is that I got a great education and also learned to become a leader—essential preparation needed every day to navigate my way through the many challenges in corporate America.

Some of this training seemed so small or insignificant at the time. But looking back now, it has been invaluable. So my point is that someone saw something *special* in me, and I challenge others to do the same.

When I interviewed the Douglass students of today, the topic of mentors was a popular one.

JLH: In your opinion, do mentors play a key role in helping college students and first-time job seekers achieve success?

Tori: Absolutely. I have three really good mentors. One I met on an airplane flight. She was about to go to sleep, but postponed her nap to talk to me. From that point on, I've felt secure in the fact that I can write her and she's there for me. Another of my mentors is a lawyer who knows a lot of people—she's awesome. Having them has been very helpful because I've been able to make valuable connections. But I really pursued my mentors: I e-mailed and called and just really showed my interest in what they were doing and let them know things that I was doing, too. And then they became interested in me. It developed from there.

Sanjana: My mentor from elementary school is still my most significant advisor to this day. When I was young, I thought she was the worst teacher I ever had. But then I won first prize for an essay among all the schools in our district—being an English teacher, that caught her eye. She'd read my papers, and in the process, we developed a great relationship. She noticed that I had very strong writing skills and would give me tips on that. I feel as if she noticed something so small [my writing], but it's now such a big part of my life. My mentor gave me the confidence to go to college, to know who I am, and feel confident about being a minority. And we're still in touch.

Jackie (senior majoring in theater arts and Africana studies): But, at the same time, it's not enough to have someone to go to. You have to find some resources yourself, do some things on your own. Still, I can't wait to find that person who will know exactly what I mean when I say, "I don't think my résumé is sharp enough" or ask, "What should I do to move forward?"

"As students, we have to support one another. I've found that as a Ph.D. candidate, my life is in constant overdrive; sometimes I find myself standing in the middle of the room spinning in circles because I don't know what direction to go in next. What keeps me sane is my network of good friends, who encourage me along the way. It makes me feel better to know that I'm not alone. They help me keep this journey in perspective."
— Delores, Ph.D. candidate

JLH: What about summer jobs and internships? Some say that they're the best routes to getting your foot in the door. Would you agree?

Vilease (senior majoring in Africana studies and public health): I think interning is very important when you're trying to be marketable, especially when you're about to graduate. It shows basic skills that you've been working on improving, be it volunteering or a paid internship.

JLH: It's a chance to relationship-build and show others in the working world that you can be responsible, from showing up on time to staying late even if you're not being paid. What do you think the other benefits are?

Lee (senior majoring in journalism and Africana studies): I worked nine to five at a media company. I didn't get paid, but it was one of the most valuable experiences that I've had in my college career. I now feel an extra level of preparedness to go into the workforce. I also met wonderful people whom I know that I can call upon after I graduate. I even got cards from some of them when I left. I didn't know that I made that type of impression, and it was a real confidence-builder.

30 Tips for a First-Class College Experience

I encourage those of you still in college to develop valuable relationships that will last long after you graduate. I say that because four years in school seems like a very long time, but it really does fly by. You'll want to keep in touch with friends and other people you've met as you build your network of contacts, for you've had a lot of fun and have shared special times with these people. When you all branch out into your individual fields, you can be a resource for each other, especially if you find yourself in the market for a job or are seeking to move into a different area altogether. These are the people who will grow and develop and move through the workforce—you'll have a special connection to them and, therefore, a good opportunity to speak with them when needed. Alumni generally like to keep in touch, so they're likely to take your calls even if they haven't communicated with you in years.

Here are 30 ways to make your college journey more worthwhile.

30 Tips for a First-Class College Experience

1. Don't limit yourself.

2. Don't let a "no" make you think you won't succeed.

3. Remember that *you* determine your own destiny.

4. Be an advocate for yourself.

5. Maintain good personal health and emotional well-being.

6. Be proactive in laying out your end goals.

7. Network—you never know where a "hello" can get you.

8. Be prepared, look for resources, and research what you want to do or who's interviewing you.

9. Be on time, whether you're a key part of the team or a temp—it impresses people.

10. Take care of yourself—don't be selfish, but nourish your spirit and your soul.

11. Be comfortable with yourself—it shows confidence— and others will be comfortable with you.

12. Smile; be polite and nice. A smile goes a long way even in tense situations.

13. Introduce yourself when and where appropriate.

14. Don't be intimidated or afraid to strike up a conversation with high-powered people.

15. Put yourself together well, from the way you speak to how you dress.

16. Stay focused.

17. Be motivated.

18. Make time for yourself—set aside "me time" to relax.

19. Be willing to take risks—go for the tough jobs, or challenge yourself to do something different.

20. Choose the path not taken—follow what's in your heart, be it a profession or a field of study.

21. If you love what you do, it's not work—it's a labor of love.

22. Don't be discouraged, no matter bad the job market may be.

23. Be positive—know that where there's one job, there are two.

24. Find the inspiration in *you*—stick up for and pick up yourself.

25. Work hard.

26. Follow your passion.

27. Develop a separate outlet aside from school or work to add balance (such as dancing, painting, or listening to music).

28. Reach for the stars—dream big, set your goals high, and know you'll get there.

29. Have faith—everything happens for a reason, despite struggles and hard times.

30. Take comfort in your beliefs, which guide you and help you to keep your eye on your goals.

   And here's one additional tip I think is great: If you have a conversation with someone and get their business card, afterwards jot down parts of the conversation or something they said about themselves, their jobs, or their hobbies. Do that so that when you call them back and reacquaint yourself with them, they'll have a point of reference *and* you'll have something interesting to say.

College can certainly be challenging and difficult at times, but it's an invaluable experience—one I wouldn't trade for anything. Those of us who have gone (or are going) to college really should take a second to appreciate how lucky we are to have had such an incredible opportunity, one that gave our journeys definition and wisdom.

CHAPTER FIVE

Your Life Story: Livingston College Commencement Address

The day I went back to college on May 23, 2002, to deliver a commencement address was a major milestone in my life. When I graduated, I certainly never envisioned myself coming back to stand on the platform with a velvet speaker's robe and tassel. But we can't always know how the joys or accolades in our lives are going to reveal themselves.

Graduations typically make me shed a tear or two because they're so full of meaning and hope for the future. This time I had a little added pressure coupled with all the emotions, and I wasn't sure how well I was going to hold up once the pomp and circumstance kicked in.

As I sat alongside deans and trustees of the university, I saw the faces of the parents who looked thrilled to see their children attain one of the greatest achievements in their lives. Some students later told me that this day was extra special because they were the first in their family to graduate from college. One young woman told me how she'd had to work full time and raise her son while pursuing her degree.

The flowers and balloons, tears and screams of joy, handshakes and hugs served to remind me of what a momentous occasion I was taking part in. And it struck me that no matter how many people you can reach in a day on TV, nothing compares to seeing them in person.

> *"Be clear on what you want to accomplish, for then you'll know whom to reach out to for help. Don't worry about what everyone else is doing, run to your own beat (running is key, as everyone else is walking), and don't look back. Recognize that you're not always going to get what you want. That's life. However, keep focused on your goal and keep striving for it—regardless!"*
> — Megan, musician

I'd been thinking long and hard about what I wanted to tell the graduates for weeks. If they were anything like *my* graduating class, I knew that a lot of the students would just be itching to toss their hats into the air rather than listen to the commencement speaker. And a lot of parents had been waiting many years for this day—so my speech had better be good. Boy, was the pressure on!

I think I took about two weeks to look through famous quotes. Then I thought about writing about some of America's most famous graduates, to try to tell a compelling story that way. But then it occurred to me that my speech was right under my nose all along. And thus, the speech "Your Life Story" was born.

Your Life Story

To the Livingston College graduating class of 2002, I salute you! Today, you have hit a tremendous milestone in your lives, and acquired knowledge and experience that no one can *ever* take away. You have worked hard, made friends, and forged bonds that will last a lifetime. Congratulations!

All 785 of you have now risen to a level that so many before you could only dream of. And being a reporter, I couldn't help myself—before coming here today, I did a little research. What I found out was truly impressive.

I knew that Livingston was founded in the '60s as a coed college that would serve a diverse student body aimed at better reflecting the racial and ethnic composition of today's society. But those are goals written only on paper. It is *you*—the students—that made those ideals come to life.

I was able to find out about the accomplishments and dedication of so many students from a multitude of backgrounds here at Livingston. All your accomplishments are to be commended.

There is honor student Melissa Velazquez, who participated in the minority mentor program. She is a James Dickson Carr Scholar and Livingston College honor student and is also active with residence life.

Corden Daley . . . lent a helping hand to Habitat for Humanity during spring break this year in Florida. Daley was recently accepted into one of the largest student-run international programs that will allow him to gain some real-life work experience in other countries.

Ali Ali is a Bridgewater Township fireman and member of the Golden Key Honor Society.

[Then] there is Jason Goldstein, who founded the Livingston Theatre Company in his freshman year—a recipient of this year's Dean's Award.

I've written thousands of stories over the past two decades. But I truly see today, this culmination of the past four years, as one of the most important chapters in *your life story.*

Let me share something else with you. I must tell you I was really somewhat overwhelmed at the thought of . . . speaking here today. Honored and humbled, yes. But, at the same time, overwhelmed.

You see, more years ago now than I often like to remember, I was just across town graduating from Douglass College—we'll just say in the '80s.

Well, I really do remember that day just as if it were yesterday. My friends walking down the path with me then are still my best friends now—nearly 20 years later. We often remind ourselves of the plans we laid out that graduation day, knowing with complete and total confidence that those plans would be etched in stone.

I was an economics and finance major. But I always wanted to write and to be on TV. My best friend, a sociology and criminology major, would rise through the ranks of administration in education. Another [friend], majoring in labor studies, would pursue accounting and later become a vice president in banking. . . . And as our lives unfolded, so did the chapters within it. There would be life's challenges and disappointments, including the jobs we didn't get, family struggles, and hurdles involved in the journey into adulthood. But the joys, accomplishments, and successes would be so much richer.

After all, it was Booker T. Washington, an African-American educator, lecturer, and statesman born in 1856, who said, " . . . success is to be measured not so much by the position that one has reached in life as by the obstacles which he has overcome while trying to succeed."[1]

We persevered, as will you. How? By keeping the focus on *your* script, who *you* are, and what *you* want to become. And you will be successful. You see, graduation day is about celebration for you, your family, and the loved ones who *all* helped you achieve your goals.

But as you look at your life story, also know that today is *so* important because you can continue on from here and build on your life's dreams.

Some of you will choose to step with both feet into the workplace, while others will go on to graduate schools, specializing in education, medicine, or law. Perhaps part of your script will be seeing the world as not only someone who lives in it—and can learn from it—but as someone who is seeking to change it for the better.

And even as the headlines these days speak of war and unrest, I still believe this is truly a great country and world we live in. But there is still plenty to be done, from helping those less fortunate to peace in the Middle East. . . . It will be your generation that will make history, having the ability to sprint into action for coming decades regarding political and social change. . . .

Think about *your* script, much like a reporter writes a story. And know that once you leave here, you will begin writing the most important chapters in your life, and there will be many.

Focusing on Your Personal Script

This speech is special to me because it applies not only to students, but to all of us—young or old, college-educated or not. If you're going to be passionate about your life, you need to keep the focus on your script—that is, your life and what's most important to you. You have the power to develop a story that's as colorful (or as plain) as you'd like it to be—you can personally create a masterpiece called "life."

Sometimes the approach has to involve taking a step at a time. I think that's why that day at Livingston was so filled with so much emotion for me. Here I was sitting with prominent educators and other dignitaries even though I was a child who had a difficult time making top grades in school. It's funny that I chose economics for my major, since I'd struggled with math since the fifth grade. My family had moved from the Midwest, where I'd been a good student and had plenty of friends, to the East Coast, where the teaching methods and standardized tests were very different. In fact, one teacher actually pushed to have me repeat the fifth grade—this after I'd skipped kindergarten altogether in my previous school.

I thank God for a mother who was a teacher and parents who believed in me and looked beyond the test scores to see what was and wasn't motivating me as a person. For a time, I was the only African American at that school—being singled out and called racially charged names did little to boost my nine-year-old confidence . . . or my grades.

My parents devised a plan to help me overcome this hurdle. I worked with a tutor, made new friends, and found teachers that were more *en*couraging rather than *dis*couraging. It was a blessing. But what would have happened if my parents had simply given up and believed that nothing would change? Would I still have grown up to wear the big stately velvet robe and give a commencement address at a college graduation?

My guess is that if no one believed in me at that juncture or worked to get me up to speed—emotionally *and* academically—I probably wouldn't have reached my fullest potential. And as painful as it was then, I like to remember that fifth-grade story now

"One must move positively through life. I keep the beat in everything in my life by realizing who I am. From there stem my traditions, my customs, and my values. No matter where I am in life, I always find myself going back to such pillars, which eventually help me to answer all my questions."
— Sravana, college student

because it reminds me that when you refuse to give up on your dreams, anything is possible.

I hope the first part of this book has helped you explore where you are and where you want to go on your career path. Now it's time to move on to the second part of our journey: health and well-being.

PART II

DISCOVERING A HEALTHIER, HAPPIER YOU!

CHAPTER SIX

From Feeling Overwhelmed to Finding Inner Peace

My journey to become physically fit has been an ongoing one; along the way, I've come to the conclusion that mental health has a tremendous impact on physical health and vice versa. That's why I felt it was so important to include a chapter on finding inner peace in this book.

I first felt the connection between the mind and body shortly after I had my second child and became extremely ill with a diseased gallbladder. Like so many working mothers, I was run-down, eating on the go, and getting little rest. Mentally, I hadn't given myself a break—nor had I allowed others to step in and take over some of the chores involved in having a new baby and an absolutely crazy schedule. And physically, I was wearing myself down. After undergoing surgery, I really had to reshuffle some responsibilities and reexamine how I wanted to treat my body and mind. And I had to become better at handling things as they came.

So many of us simply don't know how to cut ourselves some slack. In this chapter, I'll share some effective ways to stave off stress or that overwhelming feeling we often get—the one that makes us feel as if we're sinking into quicksand with our

> "Life can be overwhelming, and unfortunately that feeling can sometimes come in bunches—your husband's sick, your dad's sick, you lose your job, your seven-year-old has a major presentation at school. However, I've found a solution: Stay calm and handle things as they come. Try not to foresee the future so much. This isn't easy—it takes a lot of practice. But as the saying goes, 'Practice makes perfect.' Add a little patience, and things will work out fine."
> — Marsha, administrative assistant

paperwork, endless meetings, and countless e-mails. And then, when we get home, the kids are sick, the water heater breaks down, and our spouse is out of town. I certainly can relate to all of the above.

When I entered my 30s, I started to talk to my dad about how I was feeling about life. On more than one occasion, I told him that things just seemed to be unraveling around me.

Without missing a beat, he'd dust off some of his old jokes, which always made me laugh. My favorite was: "If you think you've had a bad day, try missing one. Now *that's* a bad day."

I'd chuckle while realizing the truth of that statement. Sure, I was having a rough day—but more important, I was living life. Every person's existence is filled with its ups and downs, but that's not a bad thing. By telling me that joke, Dad wanted to remind me that I was living, walking, breathing, experiencing, and feeling the discomfort of life in *all* its fullness.

We tend to assume that we're only "living" when times are good, we're happy, or when things go smoothly. But we must remember that sometimes being frustrated and having that weight come down around us is part of the journey, too. I've found that that frustration has often been a signal to make a change in my life or eliminate what's unnecessary and concentrate on what matters most.

Ask yourself, "What am I really overwhelmed with?" It's easy to feel deluged by our chores and the errands we have to run. But we must realize that with better organization, we can cut down on those time-wasters and focus on being with our partners, our children, or ourselves. We need to find a balance that allows us to cope with life's fast pace. We all have packed schedules— whether we work outside the home or stay at home with the kids. Nevertheless, we still need to leave a portion of it for seeking inner peace.

More and more of us are starting our day just hours after the previous one has ended. How many of us get in from work late and go to bed around midnight only to get up and start all over again at 5:00 or 6:00 A.M.? I understand that some people can function well on very little sleep. But for me, one of the most important keys to having a successful career and home life is getting proper rest. So I use the waking hours I have to get things done efficiently: I phone in orders to the bakery before going there; I make sure my dry cleaning is done before heading out to pick it up; I go to a grocery store and post office close to my home.

People often ask me how I get so many things accomplished in a day. My answer: It takes incredible organization. I really don't like to waste time—I see efficiency as a way of keeping my professional and personal life in sync. Getting a number of errands done and completing the items on my to-do list during the week means I get more free time on the weekends to spend with my family.

Here's the way I typically organize myself: In the office, I get my desk together every evening for the next day. I write myself a note or two before I leave, then post it on my desk. When I return the following day, I'm reminded of what I need to do. It may involve returning important phone calls on a story, finding videos, or going to a midday meeting; or it could be something as simple as remembering my nephew's birthday. Doing this is one way to keep some of the things I need to do fresh in my mind.

If you're trying to keep up with schedules and events at work and at home, a personal planner and a large wall calendar will help greatly. You can write down noteworthy events (such as lunch with a friend, your daughter's dance recital, or an early-morning meeting with your boss) and then transfer the information to the "family calendar." That way, each family member can add their own information, whether it's a track meet or a sleepover. Each person should write in a different color—you may use red ink, for example, while your partner writes in blue. The calendar's blocks should be big enough so that travel plans can be listed in the squares, along with contact numbers.

> *"I'm not constantly overwhelmed, but I do feel that way on occasion. When I do, I try to take some time to go on a 'throw-away spree,' in which I get rid of all the old mail, magazines, clothes that don't fit, and anything else that's cluttering my life. It really helps."*
> — Amy, lawyer

And I cannot stress the following enough: *You need to block off some portion of your day, however short, for seeking inner peace.* Pencil it in your calendar if you have to. It's that important.

I find my peace at the gym. After my first son was born, I had to deal with back problems and getting my weight back in check. I was active but lacked a set routine. Even though I was young, I found myself growing more and more tired, so I knew I had to make some changes.

The local gym was the solution. I wasn't looking for anything fancy, just someplace that I could get to every day and feel comfortable. In the beginning, my goal was to work out two to three days a week in the morning while my husband watched the baby.

I'd leave very early (around 6 A.M.), and my husband would get the baby dressed and then head out to work after I got back.

After starting my fitness routine, I immediately began to see the physical and emotional benefits. It's pretty amazing—over the past decade, my workout has blossomed into a 45-minute regimen four to five days a week. It hasn't been easy, but I've managed to stick with it, and it's really changed my life. When I'm moving and my heartbeat is revving up, I find a rhythm that allows me to unwind and, believe it or not, relax mentally. It feels great relieving tension and stress—when I don't make my workouts, my body reminds me with an added ache here and there because it yearns to be in motion. It's truly what I need to kick off a 10- or 11-hour workday.

My evenings are filled with cooking, overseeing homework, driving to football or basketball games, and preparing to do it all over again the next day—which includes laying out the kids' clothes and getting a jump start on packing their lunches. Some of my friends also pack the items they have to carry to school or work in the car the night before so that they can save time in the morning.

That tip really came in handy when I was a local news reporter. If there was breaking news, the day could easily turn into a 14-hour marathon. There were times when a jury would deliberate a major case late into the night, or a school board would hash out big budget cuts potentially impacting thousands in a community. And there were the big national news events. When President Clinton gave the commencement address at Princeton University in 1996, the media had to be in place about three hours early to allow for searches and tightened security measures.

Add to that a daily two-hour commute to work (each way).

Over the years, I've really forced myself to find ways to become more disciplined, to maximize my personal and professional time. I've been determined to make having a career and family work in tandem, without sacrificing the love, happiness, or sanity of those around me.

The feedback I've gotten from other women have let me know that I'm certainly not alone. This letter is from the mother of a pre-schooler, whose husband's job often requires him to travel.

> Dear Jennifer,
>
> It has always been a challenge for me to find the inner peace that I'm looking for. Often I'm pulled in so many different directions that time for myself is nonexistent. My survival as a working mom has been through finding "Mommy" quiet time. On at least a weekly basis, I wake up a few hours before the rest of my family, sometimes setting my alarm clock for three or four in the morning. I find a little niche of time to read, organize my thoughts, drink herbal tea, and pray. This is when I think about, without interruption, the path of my life.
>
> — Anita, math specialist

Taking Time for Yourself

Where can you find the time for yourself? As I said earlier, you need to start by writing it down, literally making space for *yourself* on your to-do list and personal planner. Just get used to the idea that finding inner peace and setting aside quiet time is essential for your overall well-being.

It doesn't matter where you are at this point in your life—whether you're a student, career woman, or mom—we all need to have our energies restored. Make an effort to alleviate some of life's stresses and shift the hectic pace to low gear *before* you start feeling overwhelmed—that way, you'll be better able to clear your thoughts and prepare your mind for the busy day ahead of

> *"I get overwhelmed often, but I find that easiest way to deal with the stress is to have 'me time.' I'll go to a café to read, take a drive and let the road lead me, or sit in my room and listen to music. I also find it very helpful to talk to my mom. Somehow, when a woman becomes a mother, she learns everything. My mother always makes me feel better— she knows how to build my confidence and how to hold me when I cry. She can see the clear, logical answer to every solution.*
>
> *"My inner peace comes from reflection. I sit back, take a deep breath, and sort through the scope of my problems— it's an invaluable practice."*
>
> — Sabrina, college student

you. Get up from your desk. Take a walk. Make a cup of tea. Do a crossword puzzle during lunch. Instead of eating in the same cafeteria each day, switch gears and head to the salad bar closest to your job.

There's a perception by many that people who never come up for air are extremely productive. That may, in fact, be true . . . but I wonder just how long they're likely to maintain that productivity level without more balance in their lives.

Big-Time Stress Busters!

It's time to think of all the different ways you can shake off that negative energy. When I'm in need of a stress buster, I have an easy fix: I'll meet with friends for a light dinner after work and hash out my problems. This always helps after a rigorous and unsettling day. I also turn on the radio or put in my favorite CD and use the drive home to help me unwind.

One of my favorite stress relievers is visiting a spa. Yet the first time I went, it wasn't even my idea. You see, several years ago, after our second child was born, my husband gave me a gift certificate for a spa weekend. I was reluctant to go, but to my surprise, it turned out to be wonderful.

Even if I can only get away once a year, I try to make my spa weekends an event. From time to time, my mother will join me. When we started going together, I didn't think of it as a bonding experience, but it really is. Ask a friend to go with you. It can be expensive, so if you need to, keep things simple. For example, do one spa service and a light lunch. Every spa is different, so find out if you're allowed to use the sauna or steam room for no added charge once your services have been completed. But definitely treat yourself. You deserve it.

What else can you do to relax? Here are some great ideas.

My Favorite Stress Busters

- **Dancing.** Expressing yourself through movement is good for the heart and the soul.

- **Laughing.** It's one of the best therapies we have for coping with a stressful day. And it's free!

- **Creating something.** Paint, do a craft, or try ceramics.

- **Writing.** Compose a poem, start that novel, or put your thoughts down in a journal.

- **Singing in a choir.** Singing uplifts your mind and spirit.

- **Ending the week with a treat**—such as a frothy, warm bubble bath. Arrange some aromatherapy candles around the room and play your favorite music.

- **Buying a new book *and* favorite brand of ice cream.** Drizzle the treat with chocolate syrup, and find a cozy spot to read.

- **Taking it easy.** Get up 15 to 20 minutes early; pick up a light breakfast and your favorite cup of gourmet coffee; and go to the park to relax, eat, and read.

- **Sitting in the sauna or steam room.** Sit back, breathe deeply, and let your tensions melt away.

- **Planning a special theme weekend.** For example, have a "New York weekend"—go see a play, stroll through a park, and dance until dawn.

Yoga—Stretching Body and Mind

One wonderful form of relaxation I love is yoga, which involves various poses or postures along with deep breathing exercises. The result is a state of physical well-being and mental tranquility.

I first tried yoga several years ago when my mother and I were on a spa weekend in Florida. I'd spent much of the time trying out new exercise machines, taking spinning classes, and doing step-aerobics classes. About halfway through the weekend, it hit me that I was really there to relax, not wear myself out. What I hadn't accomplished in terms of physical fitness before our visit couldn't be achieved in those 48 hours. Yet when my mother encouraged me to join her in an early-morning yoga class, I thought, *Yoga? Isn't that a little too low-key?* I was in for a very big surprise.

Mom and I got up early and gathered our mats and towels, finding a spot where the sunlight was peeking through the windows. The instructor put on the calming sounds of ocean waves. *Not bad,* I thought. *I'm starting to like this already.* Mom, the other beginners, and I started with a series of warm-up stretches and were told to focus on our breathing. Why? Because many of us have shallow breathing—we don't provide our lungs (and, therefore, our bodies) with the deep, cleansing breaths we really need.

Inhale deeply through your nose right now, and exhale through your mouth. Do you feel the difference between just breathing and focusing on the process—that is, letting the air come in through your nose, fill your lungs and chest, and then leave through your mouth while your entire body expands?

In my first yoga class, I became awakened to the fact that exercise doesn't have to be rigorous to be extremely effective in toning your body and conditioning your mind. Yoga challenged my body to execute poses that looked simple, but stretched muscles I hadn't used in years. The sensation of breathing and producing fluid motion was tremendous—by the end of the session, I'd fallen asleep on my mat. It was a deep, restful sleep that I honestly hadn't experienced before. I felt as if I were weightless and had morphed into the floor. I was sleeping like a baby, and it wasn't even the middle of the day.

I experienced a feeling of total peace and serenity, which was definitely an eye-opener. Since then, I've tried a number of yoga classes with different instructors. Some have conducted their sessions on the beach; others have used aromatherapy and candles. I find all of this pleasurable because it allows me to relax.

A young woman named Emma Wigglesworth was the instructor for one of the classes I took recently. In a soothing voice, Emma started her class by saying that the word *yoga* means "union"— the joining of body and mind. She said that oftentimes when we shop at the grocery store, we move the cart but our minds are off somewhere else thinking about the last episode of *Friends* or ruminating on the argument we had that morning with our mate. Yoga centers us on the here-and-now.

"Through yoga," she explained, "we use our body, concentrating on the poses and thinking about how our body responds to the movement. Instead of doing the moves and thinking about our laundry (as we might on the treadmill), we'll experience the body in all its fullness—the joy, the grace, and sometimes the discomfort.

"Yoga is very different from what we typically think of as exercise. We tend to have the 'no pain, no gain' belief in that, to keep ourselves fit, it will have to hurt. Yoga is the opposite of that—we'll draw ourselves in."

Emma went on to talk about several principles of alignment in Anusara yoga, which is quickly growing in popularity, as it combines biomechanics with the age-old teachings of yoga. "Let's focus on two of those principles. The first is to *open to grace*. You can think of grace as the spirit that illuminates. You can see this in athletes when they're playing the game they love and are performing well. You may also think of grace as a way of opening up to what's possible in your body. Take a moment to ask yourself why you came here today, what you hope to take away, and what you hope to learn.

"Now, bringing your hands down to relax on your knees, draw your spine up long. Take a moment to set an intention for yourself today. Maybe you came here to learn one new thing about your body. Maybe you want to be free of a certain pain within your body. Perhaps it's to work on loosening your hips so that it's easier to ride your bike.

"So the first principle is to open to grace, to set your intention. The second principle is *muscular engagement,* which involves firming the muscles of the body. Keep your knees bent. Make a union by pulling in and pushing out at the same time. Feel the quality of the muscle. Next, inhale. Look up as you exhale, and come back to the forward bend. Now I want you to engage the muscles of the legs and arms. Shine up through the palms of the hands to the ceiling, shining up through the bones, elongating the body.

"Always try to be aware of all the parts of the body at the same time. Any part that's in touch with the floor is your foundation, and you want your building to be as strong as possible. Again, let your body get soft, open up to something larger than you—grace or possibility.

"Take a breath. Now firm the muscles—soles of the feet to the core of the pelvis. Bring your hands together in front of your heart. Always come back to your intention, and keep your stamina up and remember what you came here to do."

It's been helpful for me to re-create these moments, thinking about my intention, what I want to achieve. The various postures allow me to channel my energy into a single thought. Among them are the Tree Pose, which is said to improve concentration, tone the legs, and strengthen the arms, and *Tadasanna* [tah-dahs-a-na], which does a number of things for the body—namely, improving one's posture and firming the abdomen.

After that first class with Emma, I decided to ask her a few questions to further learn about the ancient practice of yoga.

JLH: Why should we learn to practice yoga?

Emma: There are many reasons—the most important is that a lot of us need to understand our body and how it works. We know when our body's tight, where the bones are, and when something's out of whack. But aside from that, the connection between our mind and body is pretty foreign to us. Yoga helps us get in touch with our body.

JLH: So it allows us to understand ourselves better and the energy within us?

Emma: Yes. Exactly. A lot of us exercise, but we typically don't get very much joy from it. We don't breathe properly, or stretch, or know how to relax. Movement is such a pleasure, and a lot of people don't even realize it.

JLH: In class, you said that there are five principles to Anusara yoga. What are they?

Emma: The first two principles that I teach are opening to grace and muscular energy. Again, being open to your intention and muscular energy helps you engage your muscles, drawing you into your core, feeding yourself and taking care of yourself. The third and fourth principles help people achieve a balance or harmony that exists between them and the earth. The last principle deals with organic energy—once you've engaged the muscles, the body is aligned, allowing you to share that which is in your heart.

JLH: How can yoga help a person find inner peace, spiritually and mentally?

Emma: Yoga is a practice; it's something you do repeatedly. You're performing these specific movements that help to settle the mind over and over again. When you're aware of your body and you're comfortable in it, that leads to the sort of joy that has an effect on your spirit as well. Again, yoga is the spirit of that union, the joining of the body and the mind.

JLH: There's a word that I hear at the end of most yoga sessions: *namaste* [nam-as-tay]. Can you explain it? Is it something spiritual that we can carry with us not just through doing yoga but as a thought throughout the day?

Emma: I certainly like to say "Namaste" to my students and have them say it back to me. It means "the divine in me bows to the divine in you." When I say it to my class, I'm conveying that the part of myself—the most authentic, valuable, beautiful self—bows to all the value and beauty in you. Namaste.

> *"I find it helps to not let myself get stressed about all the things I need to do. I've learned to look at my to-do list and focus only on what really has to be done that day, those things that further the goals I've set for myself. I've learned that everything else can wait."*
> — Michelle, working mother

I hope this chapter has made you realize the ultimate importance of inner peace. And when the going gets tough, just remember: *You're no good to anyone else if you don't take care of yourself.*

CHAPTER SEVEN

Tapping In to Your Energy Source

You probably don't even know it, but you're an incredible bundle of energy—it shines and radiates out of you. Harnessing this vital energy, which the Chinese call *chi*, will give you strength and help you accomplish goals along your journey. In this chapter, I'll help you learn how to focus that energy on the things that really matter.

Power Up, Don't Burn Out

Using a tremendous amount of energy has been the story of my life, as springing into action when news breaks is what reporters do almost every day. No day is really ever the same, and I'm always racing to meet a deadline. But I've learned when to use my energy and when to save it so I don't burn out.

In my fourth year of commuting to Philadelphia from New Jersey, I knew that even though I really loved my job, I was going to have to make a change. I'd gone through one car that had about 140,000 miles on it, and was well on the way to racking up another 100,000-plus on my "new" car. If I had to, I could have driven the New Jersey Turnpike blindfolded and still would have found my way to work without a hitch.

Since my husband frequently worked in Manhattan, our family was basically stretched across three states in any given day. I'm sure it seems like a logistical nightmare, but we really made things work the best way we knew how—prayerfully, a day at a time. And just when I thought I had this crazy commute down, something happened. I discovered that I wasn't being nourished . . . my *soul* wasn't being fed.

I worked a lot of holidays and weekends, so I generally saw my children off to Sunday school, while I headed off on assignment. I had my schedule together—cooking meals on Saturday night, laying out the kids' clothes for church in advance, and setting up their Sunday-afternoon play dates. Yet something wasn't sitting right, and my energy was running low.

Yes, I had an awful commute, but there was more to it than that. I was missing the charge I got from church. In years past, attending a service helped me get through the week. I feasted on the words and fellowship, and, to a greater degree, the chance to let my hair down.

I can remember sending up a little prayer that if God could find some way for me to get back to having Sundays with my family

"Just when I think I have my chi, the beat of life changes, and I'm taught the lessons life wants to teach me. But I try to keep the beat by staying centered with family and friends—that is, sharing life's good and bad times and being there for others while still maintaining my sense of self. And as I journey through life, I hope I've learned a few short-cuts to pass along to my children."
— Joanna, stay-at-home mom

and my church, I'd be grateful. I told Him that I'd really try to be steadfast about getting more involved and tapping in to the spiritual belief that I was brought up with. This wish was so important to me that I was prepared to be patient.

A year later, my prayers were answered when I received a position closer to home. And, true to my word, I became reinvolved in my church, which feeds my soul to this day.

All of our souls need powering up in order to feel nourished. Just know that that "soul food" can come in many forms. Take the time to discover yours—the energy you save for yourself will allow you to rejuvenate the areas of your life that are important to you.

Plugging In to the Positive

Why waste your life's energy on what you can't change—the things that aren't moving you forward or don't enrich you life? Don't spin your wheels thinking about relationships that didn't work, promotions you didn't get, or money you don't have. Instead, take that energy and refocus it on ways that allow you to co-exist in a healthy relationship, take the next step up at work, or conquer financial burdens.

Go through a mental exercise with me for a few moments. I want you to consider yourself a long-distance runner. You're in a race where the "prize" is a goal you want to attain in a particular aspect of your life. You've trained and prepared for this race. You've got on your running shoes as well as your game face. You're like those powerful athletes in the starting blocks at the Olympic games. You're *ready*.

Now you certainly don't want to waste your time or energy by thinking about your opponents or those who are cheering for someone else in the stands. Instead, you should focus on your end goal—pace yourself and conserve the energy you've stored up to make it around the track several times. Then, in the last leg of the race, which is the toughest part of your journey, give it your all. Stick out your chest and drive your body across the finish line.

> *"I found my energy source in physical education when I became a certified fitness instructor ten years ago. Although I have a degree in business administration and currently work in corporate America, it wasn't until recently that I realized that working in health and fitness gave me peace of mind. I've experienced so much drama while working in the corporate world—with fitness, I release the negative and work on the positive. It's also enriched me, in that I've helped people reach their personal goals. I decided a while ago to make health and fitness a lifelong commitment. I'm truly blessed by the wonderful gift that God has afforded me, for I'm now spiritually, mentally, and physically fit!"*
> — Jocelyn, accountant

You see, in your journey around this imaginary track, it doesn't matter how long it took you to finish. It only matters that you *did* finish, using your time and energy wisely. You can apply this same exercise to "real life"—use your energy efficiently and effectively to get you where you want to go. Both positive and negative energy are powerful forces, but rarely will negative energy help you be victorious, especially when the stakes are high.

Negative energy tends to bring out emotions, causing you to react spontaneously rather than make a more appropriate decision. You may also say things to others that are hard to take back. So try to channel your energy in the best and most effective direction.

In your relationships, use positive energy to give you harmony. When you allow negative energy to take over, you weaken your union. This is what happens when you don't allow your partner to grow, aren't supportive of him, and don't let him maintain his individuality (which is what attracted you to him in the first place).

When you plug in to the positive rather than the negative, you can control your anger and find middle ground rather than simply lashing out at others. But you need to focus on your state of mind before you can do so. So, each time you go to plug in your cell phone, ask yourself, "Am *I* really plugged in?"

Synergies for Success

It's become popular for merging companies to talk about their "synergies," or the parts they have that when combined will work more effectively together. But synergies aren't limited to corporations—they're all around us and can benefit us if we're open to tapping in to them.

Think about the synergies that exist in your professional relationships: How do you fit into a group or a team at work? What do you bring to that division? Do you pull the group together, causing it to be a more cohesive, better-functioning unit?

In your personal life, the differences between you and your partner may be what cause a wonderful synergy to take place within the relationship. Perhaps he's urban and you're suburban, but each of you has a penchant for finding out more about each other's world—you want to experience the bright lights and big city, and he's looking for a little more down-home flair.

The point is that when certain energies come together, they can increase each other's effectiveness, so find ways to work with what you have in order to create the most powerful, progressive combination. That's exactly what this former newspaper executive did in a career that spanned more than five decades.

ଔ·ஐ·ଔ

Dear Jennifer,

I'm sure that I'm the oldest person you've contacted in connection with your book. My working career lasted 48 years—with the same company. Then I spent four more years as a consultant. But the wonderful part of my career was that I got to experience firsthand the tremendous changes that took place beginning in the early '70s, which made an impact on the role of women in the workplace.

I had a totally uncharacteristic mentor: my maternal grandmother. Although I knew her only through my 11th year, her spirit and sense of commitment to life in general are still with me. Her husband, my grandfather, preceded her to America by ten years, from their home in what was then part of the Austrian Empire and is now part of Western Russia. In 1902, he sent for her and their two children. My grandmother was 39 when she arrived, and she and my grandfather added two daughters (one of whom was my mother) and a son to their family.

For ten years, Grandmother had somehow managed to care for herself and two children in Europe. But once here, she realized that almost anything was possible if you worked hard enough to achieve it. Her American-born daughters married and between them had five daughters. Grandmother knew that females would need all the help they could get. I don't know how she managed to do it, but when she died (in 1935), she left behind a college trust fund for each one of her five granddaughters. She knew we had to have the education that would enable us to be financially independent no matter what. This was a lesson she'd learned during those ten years she was on her own.

I often thought of my grandmother when things weren't going well after I entered the business world. It wasn't the best of times for a female, as World War II was over, and the men were returning to the workplace. Even though I had a college degree, I had to take a crash course in typing and shorthand. But within three months, I landed a job in publishing. The managing editor of a highly respected newspaper wanted a secretary who had a journalism degree so that she'd be able to proof copy. This was a wonderful environment, and the paper was growing by leaps and bounds. It seemed as though the company could do nothing wrong in those days.

I persevered until, before I knew it, the '70s arrived. Women were finally being recognized, and in 1972, I became part of the paper's management. I concentrated on bringing young people onto the staff. Many were overqualified for the positions, but I worked with them and moved them up and out as quickly as possible. These years, when I had the chance to use my power and energy in a positive way, were most gratifying.

— Kate, retired newspaper executive

The importance of tapping your own energy resources can't be underestimated. If you continually try to stay the most positive, effective person you can be, you'll be able to accomplish anything you want—and lead the way for others to follow.

CHAPTER EIGHT

Leave Your Bags at the Door

Along your journey, you'll accumulate a lot of emotional baggage, which can often rob you of your happiness and weigh down your soul as you travel. In this chapter, I'd like you to take a close look at what you're carrying around every day, and work to get rid of those bags that are weighing you down.

Lightening the Load to See Your Blessings

Do you find yourself weighed down by breakup baggage? I find it interesting that so many of us have had relationships that lasted just a few months but took years to get over. It's important to learn to release the bad feelings and move on.

Are your bags stuffed with anger because you're still holding out on telling your sister she's got a sharp tongue? I know about this one firsthand. Once I got into an altercation with some family members, and I refused to speak to them until they apologized. But a funny thing happened—I found myself becoming more and more angry as time went on, and I actually forgot what we'd been arguing about originally. And so, I picked up the phone and dealt with the situation. Sure, it was difficult for me to swallow my pride and do this, but in the end, it felt much better than just stewing in anger.

Have you filled your bags with disappointments over jobs or promotions you didn't get? Have faith that the right opportunities will come along at the right time, even though you may not feel that the time is right. It's natural to feel discouraged at some point or another, but I've personally found that the saying "Things happen for a reason" holds true. Let me explain what I mean by this.

On our graduation day from college, my friends and I were walking in our caps and gowns toward the ceremony. We were excited as we discussed our hopes and dreams for the future. One of my friends wanted to get married and start a family right away; another was headed to graduate school. I, too, was going to get an advanced degree, but I didn't plan to marry or start a family for at least 20 years.

To my surprise, I was the first one in this group to get married and have a child—all of which happened just a couple of years after I completed grad school. These life-changing events have added a richness and texture to my life that I wouldn't have necessarily had if I'd rigidly adhered to my original plan. I truly believe that my path unfolded this way for a reason. You see, when I started my family, I focused on *them,* giving and receiving love in the midst of shaping an extremely busy and often challenging career. What I didn't know—or couldn't possibly have seen on that

"There are too many issues in life. You just have to let some of them go and learn from them. Many times I found that if I carried all that baggage with me, I'd just have a harder time emotionally. So that load had to go!"
— Monique, college student

graduation day—was that having a family would actually help me succeed. It added harmony to my life and kept me grounded. I'm reminded at the end of each and every day what is ultimately most important to me, and that's family. Success is great, but my family loves and accepts me whether I've had a stellar day at work or not.

Think again of what Emma Wigglesworth, the yoga instructor from Chapter 6, said about opening up to grace. Allow blessings to come into your life by alleviating yourself of the baggage that can block success or the gifts that are coming your way.

When dealing with baggage, it's also crucial that you take the time to look within yourself. Could you have done more to contribute to your previous relationships or in job preparation and development? If something goes wrong, is it always someone else's fault? Are you inadvertently blaming your parents for poor life preparation or an ex-spouse for whom you put your career on hold while they focused on their own? Shift the focus back to *you,*

> *"It's important to let go of the past. Every relationship is different—learn from each one—and make sure you evaluate those things in the beginning of a relationship before you get caught up in love."*
> — Suzette, engineer

and think about how *you* plan to change your situation.

Recently it occurred to me that the heaviest bags of all are those filled with grudges, which can truly get in the way of personal progress and professional achievements. You really can't reach your truest potential and feel comfortable doing so until you clean out and clear up those messy issues that have been hanging over you like a thundercloud.

As adults, we've become pretty good at masking our emotions. But I find that these negative feelings hold me back and keep my mind cluttered. I can't function at 100 percent until I feel I've communicated my thoughts to someone I've disagreed with. I need to let them know why I'm feeling hurt or that I didn't mean to hurt *their* feelings. So, if you have unresolved issues with a friend or relative, make that phone call to extend the olive branch. You'll feel better by doing this *and* rid yourself of the negative energy it took to hold on to those negative feelings. By removing this baggage one piece at a time, you can restore an important relationship.

Similarly, holding grudges will drag you down at work. Try not to be that person every office seems to have—the one who has a bad attitude and then transfers their personal problems to their co-workers. We all have our issues, but that attitude will get you nowhere. Instead, lighten your load. That's what this divorced mother of two sons did.

> Dear Jennifer,
>
> After I turned 30, I began to go through many emotional and physical changes—including anxiety attacks. The first one happened while I was having an average day at work. All of a sudden, I broke out in a sweat, felt nauseated, and had heart palpitations—I thought I was having a heart attack. I ended up in the emergency room, where I was told what was going on with my body. I knew then that I needed to make some lifestyle changes.
>
> At the time, one of my very good friends was dying of cancer. I was also in an unhappy relationship that I was trying to end. In addition, I'd spent the past four years in court with my ex-husband, battling over child-visitation issues and going through a nasty divorce. To top it off, I'd gained about 25 pounds. Needless to say, my cup runneth over.
>
> So how did I overcome these obstacles? I started by having to deal with something very difficult—the death of

my friend, who lost his battle with cancer. It was a struggle because I missed him so much. Next, I sought medical and holistic help for my anxiety attacks and began to take Xanax. I then eliminated my negative baggage: I broke up with my boyfriend, lightened my workload, and devoted more time to myself. I looked to spiritual guidance and self-help and began to spend more quality time with my children. As for the weight, it took another four years for me to drop it, but I did. I follow a popular weight-loss program as a way of life and have incorporated some moderate exercise into my schedule.

I'm now single, with much peace of mind. I'm also taking college courses—one at a time. My oldest son, who just began college, will probably have his degree before me, but that's okay. I haven't had an anxiety attack in two and a half years—however, I haven't thrown out the Xanax. Overall, I try to make the most of each day, and I'm happy with me.

— Andrea, sales representative

Carrying the Essentials for Success with You

When you look at successful people, you'll notice that there's a common thread in their lives, one of which is belief in themselves.

I noticed this self-confidence in particular in speed skater Derek Parra, who won gold and silver medals at the 2002 Olympic Winter Games. For weeks after the Olympics, there was television coverage showing Parra draped in the American flag, throwing

"One needn't bring up the past. Life's too short. Let's forget anything that made us unhappy before and live for today. Get on with the new."
— Claudia, counselor

kisses to his wife in the stands as tears streamed down his face. I couldn't wait to interview him.

In person, it was easy to see why people embraced Derek. He not only has sheer athletic ability, but he also has a wonderfully simple approach to living.

When we met, he discussed how he was managing his new-found fame. He also talked about the love he had for his wife, their baby daughter, and his family; and about having faith. He kept referring to the support he'd been given and how it was fuel for him to continue training.

When we met, what really impressed me was how he shared his dream with others, explaining how he'd managed to succeed and how he encouraged young people to do the same. After the interview, he stayed to sign autographs for the crew and let them touch his gold medal.

I definitely saw that Derek Parra wasn't weighed down by baggage. Instead, he only carried the essentials that are necessary to succeed on life's journey: a deep sense of faith that all things are possible, a belief in oneself, a strong work ethic, and the ability to pass on knowledge to others once it happens. He was a true inspiration.

Let Faith Be the First Thing You Pack

Once we've successfully lightened our load, how do we know that we're traveling in the right direction? I believe in letting faith be my compass and guide.

A young ordained pastor I know recently wrote to me on this subject.

Dear Jennifer,

What we read in the pages of the Bible is, in part, the account of how God has so lovingly and expertly woven strands of our very separate and, at times, tangled lives into a tapestry of breathtaking beauty. We can't always see the way that the knots we experience are being gently untangled by the Creator's hand and woven back again into the whole. We must have faith, an ability to trust in what cannot be seen in those moments. This requires the ability to take a deep breath and step back from the turmoil at hand, entrusting the outcome of the hands of a loving God who can take even the most horrifying of circumstances and weave some goodness out of it. Here are some passages from Scripture that speak to this activity of God as weaver . . . the promise of a loving God who sees our lives and is eager to bring us joy:

1) Jeremiah 29:11–13: "For I know the plans I have for you," declares the Lord, "plans to prosper you and not to harm you, plans to give you hope and a future. Then you will call upon me and come and pray to me, and I will listen to you. You will seek me and find me when you seek me with all your heart."

2) Psalm 139: "O Lord, you have searched me and you know me. You know when I sit and when I rise; you perceive my thoughts from afar . . . I praise you because I am fearfully and wonderfully made; your works are wonderful, I know that full well. My frame was not hidden from you when I was made in the secret place. When I was woven together in the depths of the earth, your eyes saw my unformed body. All the days ordained for me were written in your book before one of them came to be."

3) Romans 8: 28–39: "And we know that in all things God works for the good of those who love Him, who have been called according to His purpose. . . . What then shall we say in response to this? If God is for us, who can be against us? . . . For I am convinced that neither death nor life, neither angels nor demons, neither the present nor the future,

nor any powers, neither height nor depth, nor anything else in creation, will be able to separate us from the love of God . . ."
— Charlene, minister

When you're packing your bags on this journey, make them light—only allow room for new ideas, positive energy, and an optimistic attitude. When you lighten your load, and trust God to show you the way, your journey can't help but be the very best it can!

CHAPTER NINE

The Value of Being Financially Fit

I t's truly an outstanding feeling to be able to feel financially secure. Yet many of us end up having to find alternative routes on our journey because problems relating to money have put up roadblocks. I hope that the tips in this chapter will put you on the road to financial health in no time!

> *"Being financially independent is wonderful. It's one of the best feelings in life to know that you're planning for your future and releasing the negative energy that's often associated with money."*
> — Avis, civil engineer

When I was in grade school, I got five dollars a week in allowance from my parents. I also baby-sat—back then, my fee was just a dollar an hour (although some people would actually give me only 75 cents if they returned before the hour was up). If I was lucky, I'd get $1.50 from a couple who had two children. At that rate, I had to make every penny count. And I did.

I saved every cent I got from baby-sitting and my allowance. I got so good at hoarding my cash that I was sort of the Lewis Family National Bank . . . at least as far as my brothers were concerned. Even thought I was the youngest, they'd come to me for loans now and again. I was happy to pull the money from my pink piggy bank, but it always cost them. I'm not sure that I totally understood the concept of interest, but I'd lend them some spare change for a little fee. There were certainly no hard and fast rules here—I'd be happy if they paid me back and threw in an ice-cream cone.

I absolutely loved having a little stash and being able to manage it, hold on to it if necessary, or buy something I really wanted *when* I wanted, instead of having to wait for special occasions such as my birthday or Christmas.

Now that I'm an adult, my financial situation has naturally become much more complex—these days my paycheck goes toward running a household, saving for retirement, and planning for my sons' college education. But I essentially view money in same way that I did more than 20 years ago: It's something to work hard for. Money is something that you require in order to live, *and* you need to manage, save, and invest it for a rainy day.

> *"When I learned more about how to save money, it opened up so many opportunities for me. I became more confident and sure of myself—and in my ability to make it on my own."*
>
> — Mimi, reading specialist

When I speak at conferences, the most frequently asked questions I receive concern money. At one recent all-day event in New York City, I was the moderator for a panel called "Control Your

Financial Future and Sleep Better at Night." The panel's job was to help give people a financial check and overview on everything from home loans to retirement to saving for a vacation.

This topic was such a success that days later I was still receiving dozens of e-mails from attendees regarding what we'd discussed. This feverish interest made me truly understand how many people want to gain control of their finances and be relieved of the stress money often causes.

I realized that money is such an important subject because it's a tool that allows us to live out many of our dreams. Lots of people tell me that they're not necessarily trying to become millionaires, but they *do* want to have the freedom to spend more time with their families, retire early, start a business, or do consulting work. When we think about money as a tool that allows us to do things and plan for the future, we can see how pivotal it can be on our journey.

Your Financial Checkup

I'm neither a stock picker nor financial planner, but I do have a finance background and have interviewed many investment professionals over the years. And as I learned when I was a youngster, the one piece of solid financial advice that holds true in any economy, be it sluggish or robust, is this: Save when and where you can—even if it's just a little at a time. My parents' rule was always to try to save a dollar a day. I know it sounds a bit simple, but that dollar a day at the end of three years is $1,095. So you get the picture here—saving really does add up.

Now you may want to save, but you don't know how or where to find those extra dollars, especially when times are tough. So it's time to ask yourself some very serious questions—grab some paper and a pencil for a financial checkup!

How Financially Fit Are You?

First of all, ask yourself what your financial goals are and how they relate to your overall journey this year. What do you want to accomplish? Are you saving to purchase a home or a car, or do you want to finance your education?

Next, ask yourself if you're serious enough about saving up for these goals that you're willing to make some real sacrifices to make your dream a reality. What are you willing to do without? Does everything you buy have to be brand new? Are you willing to purchase a used car or shop at flea markets or consignment shops for household items or clothing?

Can you wait for a sale yet not be enticed into buying more than you need? One way to do this is to shop *before* you shop— that is, write down what you need prior to heading to the store, and *stick to your list*. If you set out to buy one CD, don't buy five because they're on sale. Get what you need and take a brisk walk out of the store. Remember that you're in control when it comes to spending your money.

If you have a spouse or partner with whom you share finances, discuss your feelings about money—what it should be used for, when and how it should be saved, and what your plans are for the money you make. If your idea of saving is having $300 a month automatically deducted from your checking account, while he thinks only going out to dinner twice instead of four times a month is saving, then there could be some tension brewing in your future. Just like any other major issue in your lives, you want to be clear and communicate how you want to use your money: Know when it should be spent on having fun and when it should be kept in savings.

If you have children, talk about the philosophy you'd like to instill in them regarding these same issues. Is it your view that money should be earned, or should it be given to children simply because they ask for it? Realize that as a parent, you're teaching lessons as part of everything that you do—money is no exception. The way you handle your finances and show that you can exercise restraint will give your kids an indication that you may have disposal income, but you prefer to save and invest it instead. I also think it's really helpful to think about the ways in which your spending habits complement your saving habits. What is the synergy there? Ask yourself the following:

1. Am I essentially debt-heavy, spending more than I earn each month and leaning on credit cards to get by?

2. Am I socking away the maximum amount that I can each pay period for savings, whether it be for college, retirement, or both?

3. Am I being prudent when it comes to buying items that I can do without?

It's not difficult to see that spending less and saving more are a powerful combination—yet we can't always accomplish that fact because there are so many things we've grown accustomed to and believe we need. So try this strategy: Again, make a list of everything you intend to buy the next time you go shopping, whether it's to the grocery store or the mall. Put a check mark next to everything that's a necessity, and circle everything that isn't. Then, put a dollar amount next to "disposable" items—add it up, and consider it savings that will go right back into your pocket.

Last, do your homework. Keep your financial records as up-to-date as your medical records. Educate yourself about the options available to you in terms of investing on and off the job. And work with professionals whom you trust and who have a good reputation—whether you're buying a home, investing in a mutual fund, or buying individual stocks.

Remember that money can be a springboard to helping you on the various legs of your journey. After all, there's a reason our parents start us out with that piggy bank—it teaches us that with careful planning, pennies can turn into dollars, and we can take control of our finances and improve our lives.

CHAPTER TEN

Winning
the Battle
of the Bulge

Like millions of Americans, I've battled my weight for most of my life. Sure, I grew up eating healthy foods, but too much of anything can be bad . . . and I really liked to eat. I also think that having been part of a generation in which fast-food restaurants and snacks were everywhere has made it tough for me to change my eating habits. Over the years, I've counted calories and have been on whatever diet was popular at the moment, from the cabbage diet to the grapefruit diet. I think a water diet of sorts may have been thrown in there somewhere, too.

I put my body through this torture until I started to get smart about my health. I began a serious routine of daily exercise coupled with wholesome eating habits. The results have been unmatched by any of the approaches that I've tried in the past—and have made my journey a whole lot easier.

And so, this chapter will focus on making lifestyle changes—not quick fixes—to achieve optimum health and fitness.

The Freshman Ten (Plus)

My current healthy lifestyle is a far cry from the way I lived in college. Back then, I'd hit the dining hall for breakfast, scooping up bagels and cream cheese, eggs, and juice. Then I'd stop back at the cafeteria to have lunch, and, of course, return for dinner. Yes, eating three times a day is a good idea—however, the portions I chose were hardly small or properly balanced.

Not surprisingly, my fellow students and I found ourselves in the same overeating boat. It was as if food was calling our name

"Weight and body image have played a large part in my life since I entered college—especially because I'm a competitive swimmer.

"I was lucky up until college to have coaches who never mentioned weight or encouraged me to eat less in order to become faster, but here, as swimmers become heavily involved in competing, it's tough because there can be a lot of emphasis on how we look and how much we weigh. Now I feel I'm at a crossroads when it comes to my weight. I've always been very confident about my appearance, but now I find myself questioning that confidence and looking to lose weight. And I'm not alone in this. I've watched four of my teammates struggle with eating disorders, which makes the weight issue even more sensitive and confusing for me.

"I realize that starving myself or indulging in 'empty' calories and junk food will rob me of my competitive edge, and I have to set realistic and healthy eating standards to take care of my body. As a member of my team, I work out 21 hours a week, so I need to eat balanced meals and plenty of healthy snacks throughout the day."

— Angela, college student

everywhere we went. The cake was seductively whispering, "Come over here," so was the ice cream and the pizza. We quickly discovered firsthand why the term "The Freshman Ten" was invented—that's how many pounds a first-year student living in the dorms typically gains, thanks to poor eating habits.

"I work late and travel a lot, which is particularly difficult for weight management. When I meet with clients, we generally have dinner—and they want me to have dessert so that they don't feel bad ordering it for themselves. I have a 'chocolate monkey' on my back, so I'll share dessert with my client instead of having my own.

"I also tend to carry low-fat snacks with me, even when I go to the movies. I bring enough for others, keeping my allotment separate. I try to track what I eat so I don't eat out of the bag. I measure a serving, then put it aside."

— Tawana, insurance executive

Yet I had a plan—I decided to teach aerobics. I organized a small group of students to meet at this clubhouse where we did our laundry. We had just enough space to jump up and down in our spandex, leggings, and headbands. Even so, "The Freshman Ten" proved to be a stubborn beast. Not only did it get in the way of me and my Calvins, it practically became "The Sophomore Twenty" by the following year.

The days of the dining hall are long gone, but I've struggled with my weight ever since. I've grown older, of course, and I've had two kids to boot. During my first ever-so-proud pregnancy, I gained about 60 pounds. I guess my philosophy was to eat anything and everything, including foods that I dreamed about during the night. I paid for that behavior because I had a really hard time losing the weight. During my second pregnancy, seven years later,

I put on about 40 pounds—see . . . I really *did* try to cut back a bit on the eating.

When I returned to work, I faced another battle: road trips. Working in the field, the crew and I would frequently grab something quick because we couldn't leave the scene of a breaking story. We'd often wolf down chips, doughnuts, burgers (or whatever was most convenient), and wash it down with gallons of coffee and soda. It was certainly a challenge to change *those* habits.

About ten years ago, I finally found the key to conquering my weight issues, once and for all—exercise. You see, I was only in my mid-20s, but I noticed that my weight was creeping up, along with my cholesterol count. I remember one of my husband's grad-school buddies asking me when I was due, when in actuality, our son had been born several months before. That's when I realized that something had to be done. I decided to join the local YMCA.

At first, it was really difficult to carve out time to work out. My goal was to go two or three times a week, squeezing it in along with all my errands in the mornings or after I'd take my son to day care. I started by walking on the treadmill for about 20 minutes.

"My weight has always been a thorn in my side. I've attempted to diet every way I know how. But recently, I've been making a concentrated effort to exercise and keep the weight off. I walk the dog twice a day, very early in the morning and when the sun goes down in the evening. During these times, I talk to God and I dream and I talk to my body. Lately I've come to realize that I have to work out, not just to lose weight, but because I reconnect to my spirit and my body when I do. My time alone is rejuvenation and edification—and I love it."

— Sadie, public relations specialist

Twenty minutes became thirty, and I started doing it four times a week. It really changed my life.

I also started to focus on eating a healthier diet, and after a lot of sweat and carrot sticks, the weight finally started to come off. Needless to say, it didn't melt away like you see in TV commercials. But little by little, my body got firmer, and I felt more confident about my body image. I'm not saying that we shouldn't love ourselves exactly the way we are, but I felt that in order to get my body more in sync with my mind, it needed some fine-tuning.

Physically, exercise made me feel stronger and more energetic; mentally, it was the stress reliever I'd been needing. Going to the gym was also a wonderful way to find a little time each and every day just for me. I had to get used to that "me time" at first, but now I look forward to it. When I work out, I condition my mind *and* my body for the very busy day that's ahead.

We need to stop looking at exercise as a punishment or a task and more as a part of our everyday routine, just like taking vitamins and eating vegetables—all part of the plan to stay healthy. The beauty of exercise is that we can all do it in some way, whether we walk, run, lift weights, or do aerobics.

A mother of two boys recently shared her "battle of the bulge" story with me.

Dear Jennifer,

As I look back on my life, it seems that my self-esteem and emotional health have been tied to my bathroom scale.

It all started near the end of eighth grade, when we were sent to the school nurse to get height and weight data to be recorded in our files for high school. I can remember the distinction of being the second heaviest girl in class. For my grandparents (who raised me since I was nine), the size of my body was considered a non-issue. For them, maintaining good grades was the important mission of my existence, not sports or extracurricular activities. Yet by the 11th grade, I was very unhappy with my appearance. So I took it upon myself to join Weight Watchers. It worked.

During college I joined a gym, did weight training, and took exercise classes—this also worked for me. However, after I got married and had two sons, my self-esteem and emotional wellness became tied to the care of my children, my full-time job, and our house. I was very unhappy with my appearance—Jenny Craig to the rescue. This worked, too, although the results weren't as dramatic as when I was in high school.

Then my family and I relocated, and I became a full-time mom. Time moved on, and so did Mother Nature, as my metabolism began to slow down. I was again unhappy with my appearance. Time to regroup once more.

Today, my current lifestyle and health habits include working out at the gym four to five days a week and watching my caloric intake. While weight management can be said to be a simple equation of input/output (the balancing of food and physical activities), it really isn't when a woman is managing a household and caring for family members. I clearly see a need to check in with myself more frequently to assess if my weight goals are on target, before my self-esteem and emotional health reach crisis levels. I've become my own manager and coach—I look at my daily workouts as medical appointments for spiritual and physical fitness that cannot be broken.

— Dominque, stay-at-home mom

Doctors would like more of us to take control of our health as Dominique has. According to statistics from the Centers for Disease Control, "Results from the 1999–2000 National Health and

Nutrition Examination Survey (NHANES), using measured heights and weights, indicate that an estimated 64 percent of U.S. adults are either overweight or obese."[1]

The CDC also says that "individuals with a Body Mass Index (BMI) of 25 to 29.9 are considered overweight, while individuals with a BMI of 30 or more are considered obese. BMI, a mathematical formula, is a common measure expressing the relationship (or ratio) of weight-to-height."[2]

Here's how you calculate your BMI: [your weight in pounds ÷ your height in inches ÷ your height in inches (again)] x 703. So, a person weighing 140 pounds and measuring 5´5˝ (or 65˝) would have a BMI of 23.3 [(140 ÷ 65 ÷ 65) x 703]. The chart below easily breaks it down for you:

Body Mass Index (BMI) Table

BMI	19	20	21	22	23	24	25	26	27	28	29	30	31	32	33	34	35
Height										*Weight (in pounds)*							
4'10" (58")	91	96	100	105	110	115	119	124	129	134	138	143	148	153	158	162	167
4'11" (59")	94	99	104	109	114	119	124	128	133	138	143	148	153	158	163	168	173
5' (60")	97	102	107	112	118	123	128	133	138	143	148	153	158	163	168	174	179
5'1" (61")	100	106	111	116	122	127	132	137	143	148	153	158	164	169	174	180	185
5'2" (62")	104	109	115	120	126	131	136	142	147	153	158	164	169	175	180	186	191
5'3" (63")	107	113	118	124	130	135	141	146	152	158	163	169	175	180	186	191	197
5'4" (64")	110	116	122	128	134	140	145	151	157	163	169	174	180	186	192	197	204
5'5" (65")	114	120	126	132	138	144	150	156	162	168	174	180	186	192	198	204	210
5'6" (66")	118	124	130	136	142	148	155	161	167	173	179	186	192	198	204	210	216
5'7" (67")	121	127	134	140	146	153	159	166	172	178	185	191	198	204	211	217	223
5'8" (68")	125	131	138	144	151	158	164	171	177	184	190	197	203	210	216	223	230
5'9" (69")	128	135	142	149	155	162	169	176	182	189	196	203	209	216	223	230	236
5'10" (70")	132	139	146	153	160	167	174	181	188	195	202	209	216	222	229	236	243
5'11" (71")	136	143	150	157	165	172	179	186	193	200	208	215	222	229	236	243	250
6' (72")	140	147	154	162	169	177	184	191	199	206	213	221	228	235	242	250	258
6'1" (73")	144	151	159	166	174	182	189	197	204	212	219	227	235	242	250	257	265
6'2" (74")	148	155	163	171	179	186	194	202	210	218	225	233	241	249	256	264	272
6'3" (75")	152	160	168	176	184	192	200	208	216	224 ·	232	240	248	256	264	272	279

Source: Evidence report of Clinical Guidelines on the Identification, evaluation, and treatment of Overweight and Obesity in Adults, 1998. NIH/National Heart, Lung, and Blood Institute (NHLBI)

Looking *and* Feeling Good

Of course, we should all rethink our eating habits in order to make more healthful choices, but when can a diet do more harm than good? That's the question I posed to veteran nutrition researcher Barbara Rolls, Ph.D., who is co-author of *The Volumetrics Weight-Control Plan: Feel Full on Fewer Calories.*

JLH: Dr. Rolls, there are so many fad diets out there. Shouldn't people be concerned about not only looking good, but feeling good as well?

Dr. Rolls: Yes. The problem with fad diets is that they encourage people to eat for reasons other than weight management—they restrict people to very few food groups. Consequently, these individuals won't get the nutrients that are important for their bodies, therefore ignoring cardiovascular and bone health. In addition, people who adhere to these fad diets don't get to enjoy the pleasure of eating, which is a shame. Also, there are so many different elements in foods such as fruits and vegetables that are shown to protect against diseases such as cancer—fad dieters may be missing out on those elements.

JLH: You mentioned the pleasure of eating. Many of us have been trained to believe that food is a sinful pleasure, something we need to have but really shouldn't enjoy.

Dr. Rolls: I believe that we should eat to live *and* to enjoy! After all, it's one of the activities that we partake in more than anything else—yet we manage to feel guilty about it. I think there are plenty of ways to eat nutritious foods that are really enjoyable.

JLH: Such as?

Dr. Rolls: Go out and pick fresh produce. In the spring, you can select vine-ripened tomatoes and cucumbers; in the summer, you can get peaches and corn; and you can buy crisp apples and squash in the fall. There's nothing better than fresh fruits and vegetables. People who learn to appreciate this will have a more positive mind-set about the foods they eat, too.

I'm worried about children not enjoying the foods that nature has given us. These days, kids are into processed foods. Our eating habits have changed dramatically over the past several years.

JLH: How can being overweight affect mental and emotional health?

Dr. Rolls: If you look around, you'll see that obesity can make people look older than they actually are. The condition can also be very tiring, making it difficult for obese people to engage in regular activities. Volumetrics teaches you to have your favorite food by learning how to choose appropriate portions of it. Just being told to eat less isn't helpful, especially when some foods eaten in large quantities help fill you up with very few calories, such as fruits, vegetables, broth soups, and low-fat smoothies. They can be eaten in large quantities and they're good for you. You can also increase the water content in foods to add volume without calories in meals such as casseroles and soups. Then you can have a few chocolates at the end of your meal. By feeling more full, you'll be less tempted to eat the entire bag of Hershey's Kisses.

JLH: Should we make it a point to be aware of what we're eating?

Dr. Rolls: Of course. Know how to select foods that are healthy, and plan up front. It's hard to eat on the go, so pack your lunch, including an apple or low-fat yogurt with your sandwich. Once you're home, don't eat leftovers just for the sake of eating them. Make a decision: Do you want it on your hips or in the waste bin?

JLH: So many of us have extremely busy schedules and need as much incentive as possible to become and stay healthy eaters. How can we get others around us involved?

<u>Dr. Rolls:</u> You can start by eating meals together as a family more often. In most countries around the world (except in the United States), that's one of the most important family rituals of the day: Everyone sits around the table eating traditional foods in a traditional manner.

I know it's difficult, but I think all of us should try to be as healthy as we can nowadays—there's no excuse not to be.

Eating Healthfully on the Go

So many of us are running in a dozen directions during the course of the day. We're trying to drop the kids off at school, tackle errands, get to work, *and* have a social life—so eating healthfully gets shoved down to the bottom of our lists.

Leslie Curtis, director of the Weight-Control Information Network (WIN) under the National Institutes of Health, recommends the following strategies for those of us with hectic schedules:

How to Eat Healthfully When You're Busy

- **Eat breakfast every day.**

- **Consume plenty of fruits and vegetables.**

- **Drink a lot of water**—limit sodas and other sugary drinks.

- **Add herbs and spices to dishes,** which will add flavor but not extra calories.

- **Choose controlled portions**—avoid those large and super-large servings.

- **Get rid of the extras**—skip thick, creamy sauces and watch the mayo.

- **Have a salad** or a grilled-chicken sandwich instead of a burger at fast-food restaurants.

- **Take ready-made low-fat snacks** with you to work, school, or elsewhere.

- **Balance your meals**—if you have a high-fat or high-calorie breakfast or lunch, eat a lower-fat dinner.

Curtis says that the USDA Dietary Guidelines encourage people to choose a diet low in saturated fat and cholesterol. In addition, she suggests that we choose and prepare foods with less salt, eat a variety of whole grains daily, and exercise—adults are supposed to get at least 30 minutes of moderate physical activity at least three times a week.

I've found it helpful to tell myself that I don't have to give up everything when it comes to the foods I love. I still have dessert or bread with butter—I just don't have it all the time. I limit such indulgences to once a week or so or special occasions. Also, if I know that I'm going out to dinner, I only have a light lunch.

During a regular workday (when it's hard enough to find time to eat), I'll make sure to bring something nutritious with me for lunch. I also find it helpful to keep a bottle of water on my desk at all times—that way, there's no excuse for not drinking it. I hide low-fat snacks in my desk or car as well—I often forget they're there until I'm really desperate for a get-me-through-the-last-hour-of-the-day snack. These snacks save me from heading to the candy machine.

> "At 63 years of age, I'm still dealing with the fat cells I acquired as a child. At age two, I was called 'Two-Ton Tillie' by unkind people. I guess they noticed that my favorite pastime was watching my mother cook . . . and eating what she made.
>
> "Over the years, as an active mother of three, I was able to maintain my weight reasonably. But now that I've retired, I must plan to exercise, drink water, and cut down on the sweets that I love. It's a constant battle, but one I must win for my health."
>
> — Monie, retired teacher

Now that we've taken a tough look at ourselves, the last part of the book will focus on our relationships with our travel companions along life's journey.

PART III

BUILDING
BETTER RELATIONSHIPS

CHAPTER ELEVEN

The Art of Communication

O n my journey, I've learned that few things, if any, are as important as the relationships we forge and maintain throughout our lives. Relationships blossom, but they require tending. Like prize-winning roses, they constantly require care, attention, and a healthy environment to grow.

In the last section of *Life's a Journey—Not a Sprint,* we'll focus on how we can be the best partner—at work *and* at home—that we can be. Let's start with learning how to listen to and communicate with each other.

Speaking Less to Hear More

Communication seems to be a simple concept, yet few of us have mastered it effectively. You see, when we communicate well, we accomplish two major things—we understand and are understood.

At home, it often takes my five-year-old to remind me of the huge significance of communicating. "Mommy, you're not listening," he'll say. Or he'll ask, "Did you understand my words?"

Once we were running errands, and my son told me that my money had fallen out of my bag onto the backseat of the car. I wasn't really listening to him, so when it came time to pull out my wallet at our next stop (naturally, I purchased a bunch of discounted items—the kind that required all sorts of extra transactions from the cashier), I was in for a shock. I had no money with me. Had I listened a bit more carefully to my son, I could have spared myself the embarrassment of standing in front of a long line of unhappy customers who had to wait as the poor cashier voided everything out.

> *"When I was married, I thought I was a good listener— after all, my husband and I always seemed to have these great conversations. However, what I realized after my divorce is that I was doing more talking than listening, and he was barely hearing me at all. It took me four years, but I'm finally back to feeling good about myself and those around me.*
>
> *"I've learned that listening truly is an ongoing learning experience—one you have to practice every day. Having kids around also helps because they demand your attention, and you have to stop what you're doing and listen to their desires. I think this is why mothers—good mothers—always know what their infants are saying. My two-year-old nephew has a lot to say, but I usually grasp only 85 percent of his conversations. Then I'll turn to my sister-in-law, and she'll say, 'Oh, he wants an apple. Didn't you hear what he said?' I typically respond, 'Oh, sorry. I heard what he said, but I probably wasn't listening as I should.'"*
>
> — Vivian, television producer

Whether people are 5 or 105, they want to be listened to, and *you* can often benefit from what they have to say. The way they communicate with you will clearly illustrate how they feel about you and what kind of relationship you have.

These days, when I ask my preteen son questions, it goes something like this:

"Hi! How was your day?"

"Fine."

"What did you learn today?"

"Nothing."

"Are you hungry?"

"Yes."

"What would you like to eat?"

"Whatever."

You can see where I'm going. I'm sure that anyone who has kids can relate to this exchange (although I've noticed that many adults often communicate in the same way). Yet whatever the person's age, I know a surefire way to engage them in conversation. With my boys, I've noticed that if I sit quietly with them long enough, they'll strike up a conversation pertaining to something *they* want to talk about. This way, I find out what they're interested in—music, movies, clothes, and even current events and books. These icebreakers are essential when you want to be more in tune with your children.

In work settings, the same holds true: Ask your co-workers about their families and hobbies and you're likely to get a favorable response. After all, people want to feel that you're genuinely taking an interest in who they are.

The reason I'm making such a fuss about communicating is because it helps us in just about every aspect of our lives. We have more satisfying relationships when we feel we're being listened to and we can speak openly about our feelings and desires. We build stronger ties to our children, siblings, and parents when we can truly empathize with them instead of just speaking at them in a one-sided manner. At our jobs, it's essential to sharpen these skills, because most of us work among a network of people.

"There's no question that I can outtalk most people. I love to share my views on the world and engage in healthy debate, so it takes real effort for me to stop and "actively" listen—that is, with my ears and my eyes, since so much of communication is nonverbal. But I've learned to listen, and it's helped in so many ways. First, I actually hear what people are saying. Second, I'm a more compassionate person because I've learned to really tune in to other people's thoughts and problems. Through being a better listener, I've made better relationships—people feel more confident speaking to me now that I listen more and speak less."
— Donna, insurance executive

At a television station, changes occur so rapidly that everyone has to rely on one another. In a live show, I work with camera people, floor directors, TelePrompTer operators, producers, and directors. Things would fall apart very quickly if we didn't keep each other abreast of changes—a video mistakenly disappears, the microphones weren't sound-checked, and so forth. Communication ensures smoothness even in the midst of what may look like organized chaos to most people.

Remember, the key here is to know when it's best to listen. I know it seems like an unusual piece of advice coming from someone who makes a living by talking several hours a day, but it's a skill we should all employ if we want to be more compassionate and focused on learning about those around us.

Here's a note from the mother of three grown children who's gleaned some important tips concerning the value of being a good listener.

Dear Jennifer,

In the last 26 years of my life, I've seen a major shift in the way we communicate. Books and magazine articles have appeared that encourage wives to make their needs and preferences known to their husbands (and vice versa to a lesser degree). Marriage-enrichment programs, role-playing, and weekend retreats have been an aid in teaching many American couples and families how to communicate more effectively.

Parents and children can now learn how to dialogue with one another. Keeping these lines of communication open is extremely important for a good relationship. Our children need to feel comfortable sharing their thoughts and feelings so we can help them through a crisis. They must be taught to express themselves as well as listen to others.

After raising three children, I found that I had to communicate in a different manner with each of them, depending on their personalities. Most of the time, I "listened" to them by observing their body language—especially as they became teenagers.

Identifying feelings is a skill that takes years to learn, so we must be patient. Taking time to listen is essential in order to have and build good communication. Here's what I suggest:

1. Communicate regularly.
2. Make an appointment to talk privately with the other person in a quiet environment.
3. Always give the other person your undivided attention. Let them know that you appreciate their sharing, especially if the issues are critical.
4. Don't speak in a harsh manner, or the person may tune you out. Use simple vocabulary, and above all, relax by taking calm, deep breaths.

        — Phoebe, retired teacher

When it comes to listening to someone you have a relationship with, I also suggest the following:

1. **Give the person you're communicating with your full and complete attention:** Make eye contact and be quiet—this way you can understand their questions or allow them to make their point during the dialogue.

2. **Give yourself a moment to think before you respond,** especially in tense situations or serious conversations.

3. **Be in control of yourself** and where you'd like the conversation to go: Quietly assess what the other party has to say and maintain your composure, even when you disagree with them.

4. **Know that your body language is as important as the tone of your voice:** Be sincere and honest, but don't allow your physical emotions to overshadow some of the thoughts you may convey. For example, if you're saying "I'm sorry," make sure that your arms aren't folded across your chest while you look out the window.

5. **Think briefly about the way you'd like the conversation to end:** Do you want to continue to have an open dialogue with this person? Are they key to your office, or are they especially close to you personally? Know that the way you end this conversation may create a lasting impression as far as how your relationship will be with this individual in the future. Think about how you may need or have to communicate with them down the road, whether it has to do with a project or an important family matter. Think about it—you may need to keep the gateways to communication open, even when you don't feel like laying eyes on this person ever again.

How Listening Well Speaks Volumes

How many times have you called a friend, not because you wanted to talk but because you really wanted them to listen? My girlfriend and I used to say that we could have great conversations with a tree stump, we love to talk so much. But knowing when it's time to listen can be an invaluable skill.

> *"People only care how much you know once they know how much you care. When you actively listen to people, they start to care and feel comfortable with you. You become real to them, and they'll want to develop a relationship with you."*
> — Marjorie, staffing consultant

There have been a number of times when a restaurant server has sat down with my family at the table to hash out a problem with me. It may be annoying to some people, but I really don't mind. If anything, I'm always surprised that people confide in strangers. Don't get me wrong—of course I want to have a quiet intimate dinner as much as the rest of the world every once in a while. But listening to these people has helped me hone my listening abilities. Now I use silence to deliver the exact messages I want to convey. Not speaking is effective especially when I'm tired and don't feel like opening up, or I'm angry and feel that it's best if I just control my tongue, or I'm having a serious conversation that requires me to be firm yet professional.

Words are powerful. You should think carefully about what you want to say *before you say it*. On the job, listen to the terms your bosses use to describe you in your reviews. Are they saying things like "Your work is progressing" (which means that you'll probably only make lateral moves throughout the company, if at all)? Or are they saying you're on the "fast track" and have an "outstanding reputation"? Also pay attention to the tone of the conversation and the body language of the person talking—this will give you some very clear signs as to how comfortable they feel with you and the information they're delivering.

> *"When I was a peer facilitator, I learned that it's very important to listen more and talk less. When you do, you allow people to open up to you, and they feel more comfortable around you. It's helped me greatly because I realize that sometimes people don't want me to give advice or put my two cents in—they just want to be heard."*
> — Tammy, college student

When you stop and listen, you'll open yourself up to receive crucial information from other people. Consequently, everyone wins—they'll feel more comfortable opening up to you, and you'll benefit from a deeper connection. And that connection is what fulfilling, lifelong relationships are based on.

CHAPTER TWELVE

Love

Love: The Beatles, Tina Turner, and Celine Dion are just a few of the people who have sung about it over the years. It seems as if our culture just can't stop talking about love. And why would we want to? After all, love is like the energy that a sprinter uses to run a race—it charges us and fills our bodies, allowing us to dash to the finish line just as we're wondering if we have enough strength to take another step. When we have love in our lives, it makes us feel incredible.

Our journeys become much more satisfying (and fun) when we forge special connections to other people. This chapter explores the subject of love—and the powerful effect it has our lives—in further detail.

Finding Power in Loving Yourself

The most overlooked but critical love is that of the self. When you look in the mirror, what do you see? I'm not asking if you have a pretty face—what I want to know about goes deeper. If you realize that you're a vessel with a purpose on this earth, then you should really love what you see. Each of us is here for a reason and has a contribution to make, no matter how big or small—so knowing that you're a person with a purpose is a powerful reason to embrace yourself!

Have you ever taken a close look at people who don't love themselves? They're angry, unpleasant, or disgruntled, and they want others to be the same. Since they don't love themselves, they can't love anyone else. And it's a shame, too, because when somebody gives love, it comes back to them tenfold.

"As a child, I was sexually abused, and for a long time, I considered myself unworthy and 'different'—how could I be like everyone else if something like this happened to me? It took me a while to figure out on my own that the abuse wasn't my fault. I was 21 before I told my mother, although she'd suspected and had even asked me about it. But I lied to her. Instead, I dealt with all that anger, hurt, and shame on my own, talking to no one but God and feeling angry with Him. Finally, I opened up my eyes and understood that I can use my experience to help other people. The strength that I took away from my this lets me know that I can do anything. I'm powerful. That's such a big statement. Power isn't something that you work up to, it's something that you possess, have to accept, and then use. And it's given me the ability to love myself again."
— Monica, graduate student

When you love who you are, it shines through. By the same token, when you love what you do and are enthusiastic about your work, people can't help but notice. When you use kind and loving words when speaking to those around you, that's the way they'll speak back to you. When you have hobbies that excite you, you're a happier person. And when you give of yourself—participating in that blood drive or helping out in the soup kitchen—it shows that you care. Love is something that can infuse every aspect of your life, and it all starts from within.

Wholesomely Loving Someone Else

Once you love yourself, you can wholesomely love another—that is, you can give to someone else without the expectation of always getting something back in return. You feel strong and capable and can bring that to another.

Loving someone goes well beyond the intense passion of being "in love." It's about being kind, considerate, and unselfish. Wholesome love is very profound. You'll feel inspired to reach your dreams—the little ones and the big ones. You're a player on a team, so you'll support and encourage each other in all that you do. It's easier to be your best when you have someone beside you who's sincere and has your best interests at heart.

If you're on this "Love Team," you should be your partner's biggest fan. When you feel this deeply about someone else, you'll be able to help them achieve things beyond belief. For example, this wholesome love allowed me to be secure in the knowledge that, even though I was a young mother, my husband would support me as I avidly pursued a career not known for job stability. For years I worked weekends, nights, and holidays, and he still encouraged me to hang in there and let my journey unfold—as a woman, a mother, *and* a reporter. That's love.

Love gives you a foundation on which to grow. And it helps you attain heights that you may not have even known you could reach on your own. I recently received a letter from a newlywed who perfectly illustrates this concept.

"Like the nursery rhyme says, 'First comes love.' Yet _keeping_ love relationships on a good note can challenge emotions and energy levels. Remembering why I married my husband and recalling our romantic pre-marriage relationship has helped me continue to nurture our union over the years.

"Don't forget to spend time together, just the two of you. Don't hesitate to get a qualified baby-sitter so that you can have evenings, weekends, or other time alone. My husband and I once revived ourselves with a three-day trip to New York City to wine and dine and attend the theater. Our son was almost two at the time, and believe me, we needed to get away.

"Love your children, but love your man, too. After all, when the children are gone, it'll just be the two of you again—you don't want to wake up and realize that you're now married to a stranger."

— Willie Mae, school administrator

Dear Jennifer,

Next month, I turn 30. I told my husband I wanted to celebrate by having a big party—not because it's my birthday, but because I've found my soul mate. Feeling fulfilled as a person has come from finding happiness.

As a child, I was unable to find that happiness. I struggled in school, and my parents and teachers didn't know if I was lazy, disinterested, or suffering from a learning disability, but they tried to find me help. I was in resource classes and constantly pulled out of class to go to "special" teachers for help. In addition, I had tutors outside of school. Even though this continued even through high school, my social life was great—I had friends and participated in extracurricular activities.

When it came time to pick a college, I met with my guidance counselor, who gave me some news I didn't like. She said I wouldn't be able to get into a four-year school—I should try a junior college. I wanted the living-at-college experience, so I went to another counselor who told me about other colleges. I was accepted to Kean University in New Jersey, where I worked hard and studied like crazy. But when the first-semester grades came out, I only had a 1.4 grade-point average, so I was put on academic probation. I was beside myself—I've never cried so hard in my life.

Then I met John. He was fun, nice, and very cute. Our relationship blossomed as we fell in love. Spring came, and so did grades—this time, I did great. Then I was talking to one of my friends about the future, and she suggested that I look into art education. That was when the lightbulb went on: I'd always loved art and I wanted to teach. So I became an art-education major, and with the continued support of John, I was ready to fully commit to my education.

I started weaving baskets, building things out of wood, and painting. In fact, I found that I had a passion for oil painting—I took painting classes and improved every semester. I was even asked by one of my professors to put one of my pieces in an exhibit at the college. I was thrilled. I graduated from college never having made the dean's list (but I did come very close), yet I was very proud of myself. Everything was finally clicking. I'd found my niche, and it was a combination of two things—art and John. Is it possible for someone to be your niche? I think so. John has allowed me to believe in myself—he's given me the confidence I needed to become a better student and artist.

This is my sixth year as an art educator, and I love it so much that I almost can't believe I'm being paid to do it. I'm also in my final phase of graduate school—I'll soon have my master's degree in fine-arts supervision.

I've finally found happiness. Thank you, John.

— Sherry, art educator

Congratulations are in order for Sherry, for she's found a way to enjoy complete harmony in life—including success in a career that she's worked very hard to attain and a relationship with a loving, supportive spouse.

As you can see, having someone to travel with you on your journey can make it that much sweeter, as you can celebrate together when the road is smooth, and you have somebody to lean on when the going gets rough.

CHAPTER THIRTEEN

Marriage

We've all heard the staggering statistics: More than half of all marriages in the United States end in divorce. It would be tough to find anyone who says that marriage doesn't have its ups and downs . . . so how do you keep the flame for your spouse burning bright? Having been married for almost 20 years myself, I'm the first one to admit that matrimony isn't easy. However, in this chapter, I'll give you some hints on how to make this part of your journey as smooth as possible.

My Engagement Story: Who Popped the Question?

If you let my husband, Joe, tell the story of our engagement, he'll say I asked *him* to marry me; I say he's the one who proposed. Here's what happened. One night I flew into New Jersey after completing the final portion of my grad-school program in Washington, D.C., and Joe was *really* late picking me up. He'd told me that we'd be going out, so there I was, the last one standing at baggage claim, all dressed up and watching my suitcase going 'round and 'round on the luggage carousel. When he finally showed up, he had a dozen roses in his hand, but all I could notice was how nervous he was. He looked like he was going to pass out. And when we got in the car, he couldn't remember where we were going. I knew then and there that something was up.

We finally made it to this very elegant Italian restaurant. There were candles and a piano player and champagne, lobster, and steaks. It seemed as if that dinner took forever. About two hours later, as we were finishing our meal, I could see bright lights out of the corner of my eye. A group of waiters was carrying a large cake strewn with candles in my direction. This was a little confusing, as it wasn't my birthday. When the servers placed it under my nose (as dozens of other couples watched), I looked closer. Underneath the flaming candles were the words *Will you marry me?* written on an ornate butter-cream cake.

The moment was so emotional that all I could do was bury my face in Joe's chest and cry. I was in awe and shock at the same time. Here I was: I had the perfect guy, and we were deeply in love, but there was one little problem—I was just 23. This wasn't part of my plan! I was going to get married in my 40s, didn't he know that? This was really screwing me up! *Settle down now?* I thought. *I'm just ramping up!*

I never did give Joe an answer that night—I told him we'd have to discuss it further. Weeks passed without either of us bringing up

> "I met my husband when I was 17 and he was 19. He proposed after 11 days, yet we've been married 45 years! Our marriage has endured because of our commitment to each other and our willingness to accept each other's differences. We worship together, laugh together, and give each other space to pursue our own interests."
> — Monica, retired teacher

the subject again. And then he dropped the bomb on me: He announced that he was leaving and thinking about moving on. I probably shouldn't have taken him too seriously, but I was really upset.

Shortly after he broke this news to me, I asked what it would take to make him stay. He took that tender moment and ran with it. The conversation went something like this:

"What would it take to make you stay?" I tearfully requested.

He was really acting now. "Stay—as in permanently?" he asked.

I replied, "Yeah, stay as in a long time."

"So you want to marry me!" he exclaimed with a smirk. "I accept!"

To this day, he tells people that I asked him to marry me. And every time he says that, I smile.

Just like babies, marriages don't come with instruction manuals. However, Joe and I went through premarital counseling, which was required by our church. I think it really helped, since it gave us some food for thought about how to communicate and how to go about clearing up conflicts.

And no matter how it happened, I've never regretted my decision to chuck my plans and marry Joe when I did—it certainly made life interesting, but isn't that half the fun?

Communicating After Your Wedding Day

Weddings are certainly exciting and emotional, and much thought, preparation, and money goes into them . . . but they only mark the beginning of marriage. Much of what you'll learn about each other as husband and wife comes after the big day—when the reception's over and it's just the two of you.

If you've found that you're in a post-newlywed funk, take some time to sit down and ask each other the following questions: "Are we still communicating? Do we still share common interests? Do we continue to inspire each other? Are we making the sacrifices needed to help each other realize our dreams? Are we willing to be creative to make sure that we really enjoy the time that we spend together?"

Also ask these two tremendously important questions: "Do we still feel that we're each other's soul mate?" and "Do we feel a connection so strong that words could describe it but not quantify it?"

Be honest with each other, and really listen to what your spouse is saying. These kinds of conversations can really help you pinpoint the areas of your union that need a little extra attention.

> "I've learned that the wedding is just the ceremony, and the marriage is the lifelong journey. Commitment to each other and sincerity in making vows are both the beginning and integral parts of a successful marriage. When difficulties arise, this firm foundation (and faith and trust in God) will see you through."
> — Liz, financial advisor

Today, people are coping with intense careers (long hours, arduous commutes, and constant travel) and raising families on top of managing a marriage. I'm sure my house isn't atypical in that we go through football, basketball, and track seasons, and our younger son takes gymnastics and swimming. In addition, Joe and I both have hectic jobs. So where do we find time for the romance? The conversation? Well, we really have to make time for each other. We try to keep in mind that in between all the things we want to do for the children, we're still a priority for each other.

Recently, I spoke to Alvin Poussaint, M.D., about how we can all keep our marital fires stoked. Dr. Poussaint is a professor of psychiatry at Harvard Medical School and director of the media center at Boston's Judge Baker Children's Center. He was also a script consultant for NBC's *The Cosby Show*.

JLH: Dr. Poussaint, you worked very closely with Bill Cosby and the cast of *The Cosby Show*. Is it really possible for people to believe that they themselves can have that wonderful balance between home, life, and work like the family on the show had?

Dr. Poussaint: One of the things about the show was that you got to see a sprinkling of the parents' work world—yet they were generally home in the evenings. The show stressed parental involvement. Bill Cosby's character emphasized the importance of being a good father and being involved with the children—it wasn't just the mother's job.

The family existed in an atmosphere of love and nurturing. The parents were respectful of the rights of the children even though the parents were the authorities. The children could come to their parents and talk. The communication was the connection.

JLH: What advice do you have for couples who feel worn down in their relationships and want to get back on the right track mentally and spiritually?

Dr. Poussaint: So many people complain about being overburdened and seeing their relationships suffer because of it. Ultimately, many divorces are the result of people being pulled in so many directions. One thing that couples have to realize is that they have to compromise and have patience. And they must realize that things aren't going to be perfect—there are going to be strains and stresses and sometimes disagreements. It's critical that the couple talk about things so that issues don't smolder and stew, and they don't build up a lot of anger.

JLH: I find it's easy to argue about simple things, such as who's going to do a particular chore or errand around the house. Is that normal for most couples?

Dr. Poussaint: Yes. Disagreements may involve how much a person is sharing in the raising of the child or in household responsibilities. Realize that chores can be shared depending on what people feel comfortable with—if the husband knows how to cook, that's the chore he should do. Or if someone likes grocery shopping, that person has to bend. You need to be flexible.

JLH: How can couples use the that good feeling that goes along with having a cohesive unit to their advantage in other areas of their life, especially work?

Dr. Poussaint: Love is a "natural high." If you're feeling satisfied in an intimate, loving relationship, it's much more sustaining and makes even the stresses easier to bear. But I think that couples have to realize that romantic bliss changes, and they shouldn't see it as a failure. They should expect that at times there will be certain strains. One person may be fatigued or under a lot of tension and they may not feel like having sex for weeks at a time. The other partner needs to be understanding and know that there are ups and downs in any long-term relationship. Couples come in to see me and say they want a divorce because they're "bored" with each other. By that, they mean they're not on that "high." Yet who can sustain that for ten years? Couples have to keep refueling their relationships—I suggest that they try being creative and playful.

JLH: For those of us who have families, what can we do to lessen the tension and make our households run more harmoniously?

Dr. Poussaint: Be organized. Make the best use of your time, and cut down as much as possible on doing extra things at work that keep you away from home. If your children are with a babysitter all day, and you don't get home until six, you may be spending just two and a half hours with them during the average day. You have to reserve as much time as possible for your children. I suggest the following:

- Recognize that you can't go to every social engagement.
- Accept that you're going to have to make sacrifices to be with your kids.
- Talk to your kids, do things with them, and help educate them.
- Think about where you can take your children, and do activities together.
- Find a good day-care provider who can make a long-term commitment (so there's little turnover).
- Find a sitter who's warm, caring, and reliable and who understands your values.
- Be patient.
- Do the nurturing things, such as giving baths, reading stories, and so forth.
- Consider a flexible schedule to spend more time at home when your children are young.
- Look to your extended families for help and support.

Dr. Poussaint: There are a number of lessons throughout life that need to be learned, and then revisited from time to time, in order to have healthy relationships. When I feel that I'm overwhelmed and out of touch with my wife, I try not to let that manifest itself.

Also, when you know that you're not talking enough, or you spend "date night" dinners out only discussing the "wee ones," it's time to go on a weekend getaway or an overnight stay at a nearby hotel. Sometimes it's necessary to remember why you're together in the first place—refocus on the things that drew you to one another.

> *"In marriage, love is vitally important, and it eventually turns into respect for each other. It takes continual effort to make one's marriage successful and enduring. No one person should have to do everything—whatever needs to be done, you both should do it. And remember: 'Love is kind and abideth forever.'"*
> — Susan, executive

Dr. Poussaint is right on the mark in saying that marriage requires energy and a constant juggling act. My husband and I try to spend enough time with our children, but we work very hard not to lose sight of each other in the process.

Ultimately, it's okay to realize that you can't "go it alone." When friends offer to take your little one to the movies along with their own children, seize the opportunity so you and your spouse can go out to dinner or take some quiet time to recharge your batteries. You deserve it.

> *"Marriage is an eternal dance of thoughtfulness, tenderness, caring, and sharing. My mother, who was married for seven decades, taught me that. She said healthy relationships are steeped in giving and receiving in limitless amounts, more than a husband and a wife even know are possible."*
> — Victoria, retired social worker

For advice on this subject, I tend to look to my own parents, who have been married for 48 years. They certainly have had their share of challenges and triumphs. Early on in their marriage, my dad, who rose through the ranks of the U.S. Treasury Department, worked as a young undercover drug agent. He broke the color barrier back then, but needless to say, the assignment was dangerous and stressful. There were many days when the family had to be protected by police because of the nature of the drug bust or surveillance operation he was working on.

At the time, my mother had two babies (my brothers) and was living away from her family. She needed to be strong and have a lot of faith that her husband would come home each night alive and well. By the time I came along, Dad was pretty successful, receiving promotions that required us to move around the country. My mother was supportive through each and every juncture of his career. Their lives are a good example of the give-and-take that marriage often requires.

I remember my father telling me as a teenager that it's important to marry someone who's flexible and able to adapt to the changes life brings. My mother added that a good spouse should be enthusiastic and caring. I think a combination of both is what makes a well-balanced relationship. But before any of that can happen, sparks have to fly.

My parents initially met at a basketball game in 1953. My dad was dating someone else, but my mother caught his eye. They went out on a few dates. Still, he didn't have a lot of time to get to know her that well because he was drafted into the Korean War as an interpreter. He spent two years in the Army, and from the day he went into the service, he started writing my mother love letters. He sent souvenirs from abroad, including silk screens and kimonos— gifts she still has to this day. She told me that his letters were really special. "I guess I knew then that it was love," she said.

Three kids and a lot of grandsons later, I guess it shows what's attainable when people are willing to respect each other, work together, and care for each other through thick and thin. I think they're an inspiration for all of us married folks.

CHAPTER FOURTEEN

The
Baby
Carriage

A long our journey, some of the biggest joys—and challenges—come in the smallest packages. That's right, I'm talking about our kids. They frustrate and worry us . . . but would we trade them in for anything? I don't think so. This chapter relates to our favorite pint-sized individuals.

A Special Delivery That Changes Life in an Instant

Having a baby single-handedly moved my life to a totally different level. I can vividly recall the moment they handed me my precious little boy for the first time. I felt an entire range of emotions—from sheer fulfillment and exhilaration to fear.

The next day, as Joe and I dressed our newborn in matching everything—hat, outfit, blanket, car seat—you name it (as all first-time parents do), I noticed that the excitement we'd felt just the day before was rapidly dwindling. When it came time to wheel me out of the hospital, I thought about grabbing on to the bed railings really tight because I wasn't ready to go yet.

Then we got in the car. Joe and I had packed up all the balloons and gifts, but no one had included instructions on how to care for a real live baby. Sure, we'd taken Lamaze classes (although Joe always fell asleep during the parts that required us to take deep breaths and relax) and had read all the pregnancy classics by authors such as Dr. Spock and Penelope Leach. However, we were still pretty nervous about the new frontier called "parenthood."

As we drove home, my husband said very little. I didn't have much to say either except "Take me to my mother's, please," even though she lived an hour away. It was the longest ride I have ever taken. Joe looked at me, I looked back at him, and the baby was looking at the both of us as if to say, "Do these people really know what they're doing?"

Since then, parenthood has been a work in progress, involving a lot of tears and prayers along the way, laughter, too—our children have been the ones to make Joe and me realize that there are very few things worth going to bed angry over. And as conservative and adult as we are at work, our kids make us growl like lions and hoot like monkeys when we get home.

Of course, we've also had to learn how to become Santa Claus and the Tooth Fairy. In fact, out of all the different roles I've played in my life, the Tooth Fairy is probably my favorite—although it's a challenge nabbing a tooth the size of a pea from underneath a little boy's pillow. One night I almost fell short of my duties. At 1:00 A.M., I was ready to turn in when I remembered that I hadn't written my note or drawn the giant tooth I customarily make for the Tooth Fairy. So it was back out of bed and down to the kitchen, where I keep my Tooth Fairy stash. I was all set . . . but when I went to get the "goods" under my son's pillow, I couldn't find the tooth. I actually had to go back downstairs and into the garage to find a flashlight so that I could quickly peek under the pillow and locate his tooth. All of this took well over an hour, and I just had to laugh at myself.

While I'm the one who looks for teeth, my husband is known for fixing boo-boos. He generally uses the biggest towel he can find for the tiniest scrape. I guess the idea is that it's got to make a five-year-old feel better if his arm is wrapped up in a homemade sling half the size of his little body. And slight shiners on the forehead call for a head wrap (imagine a kindergartener looking like he's just come from the spa). Being a great stand-in for Santa Claus, my husband has also eaten more than his fair share of cookies on Christmas Eve—which would probably be a treat for most people, but as the manager of a Fortune 500 food-and-consumer-products company, he's made his living out of making cookies.

There's something to be said about having children many years apart. Ours are seven years apart, so I've had to learn the correct form for writing the letter *M* all over again, while at the same time—at the same table—my oldest son is grilling me about molecules. No wonder parents are so tired at the end of the day!

Even so, there's nothing that I'd rather do than share these moments with my kids. People often ask me how I manage my busy schedule, and I'm afraid I don't have a secret key to "having it all"—it's truly just a balancing act that requires careful planning. I encourage people to use their support system or develop one. Call on the kids' grandparents, godparents, or aunts and uncles for help. And let your children know that they're loved and supported, no matter what your particular work schedule may be. They need to know that you're behind them 100 percent.

"My main theme centers on support. I've learned that we're all in this life together—we're not meant to suffer alone. Support adds strength, direction and, yes, help. And we all need it. To yearn for a community who understands and is eager to be there for you and your family is natural and normal. Finding a support network is amazing!"
— Nicole, lighting director

The question I get asked the most is: "How do you keep going, especially since you have kids?" The answer I give is that being a good parent *and* committed to your profession aren't mutually exclusive. When you plan the best that you can and remember what you want to accomplish, your energy will rise to the occasion. And that energy will help you through those days when you're tired, the teacher calls you at the office to ask about your child's missing homework, and your other kid is under the weather.

For me, the roughest part of parenting the first time around were the trips to the hospital—when my oldest son was an infant, he had to have surgery, and there were also many emergency-room visits for high fevers and infections. But through it all, I learned to be prayerful and prioritize what needed to be done first and foremost, which was to focus on my child. I had to learn to not be afraid of losing my job or feel that I was inadequate in some way because I had a sick little one to care for. *Will this put me in a negative light with my boss?* I'd worry. *Am I less of a team player because I've gone through so many sleepless nights? Is my head less in the game than someone else's because I'm a mom?*

I learned to release these thoughts, taking stock in knowing that I was a good worker, had shown that I had an excellent command of my job, and had gone above and beyond the call of duty when asked to pitch in for the team.

I realize that I actually owe much of my career success to my kids. Becoming a parent has helped me push beyond the limits that others said were possible. I want to leave a legacy for my children; therefore, I feel compelled to live out the dreams I have for myself so that they can see what's possible. Thanks to them, I can be multifaceted and wear many hats in my professional life. And my sons allow me to see what the true test of having patience is all about. All of this has helped tremendously in what I do and how I interact with people from all walks of life.

Still, there are plenty of times I question myself as a parent. I often wonder how I can keep going, and how I can accomplish one more thing. And having a job that requires me to be away from my kids most of the day (and go out of town on a monthly basis) has caused me to experience pangs of guilt on more than one occasion: *Am I failing my kids? Am I a failure as a parent? Am I doing the right thing?*

The truth of the matter is that your children will love you as long as you do all that you humanly can to show them that you're there for them. If your work requires you to travel a lot, say, "I'll be there when you need me—no matter what." Then when duty calls, be prepared to prove it.

Reaching Out and Keeping in Touch

Now that I have a preteen, I simply have to reach out and corner him sometimes just to find out where his head is and how he's feeling. I've seen how important it is for me to make time just for the two of us.

I'll take him out to breakfast or drag him shopping, or *he* takes *me* when it's time to buy his size 12½ sneakers! But for now, it really doesn't matter what we do, so long as we do it together. It's nice. And with preteens having so many issues to face these days, our time together is vital.

> *"Raising my kids is my current career choice. Here are some of my strategies for success: Have an accurate calendar, a telephone list of playdates, a creative imagination for rainy days, an outlet for self, a sense of humor, a cup of tea, and at least one good friend to use as a sounding board."*
> — Judy, stay-at-home mom

Besides giving each child some special time alone with Mom or Dad, it's been crucial for my husband and me to provide "working systems," or ways to make it easier to be in touch with the kids whether we're at work or traveling.

I make it a point to call home at roughly the same time each day, which my kids have grown to expect. They're also always free to call me to check in after they get home from school. In addition, I have a "hotline," or a number that I've asked my children to call in a crisis and *only* in a crisis. And so they know that I can always be reached, and even though I work, they can count on me.

My husband, who travels quite a bit, has devised his own way of keeping in touch with the boys. He makes it a rule to call the kids shortly after dinner to check in on school assignments and find out about their day. Sure, I check over their homework and projects and read over reports in the evening or prepare for show-and-tell— but my husband came up with the idea of installing a fax machine so that he and our oldest son can always review complicated math and science homework together. I'm available, of course, but my son can also fax, e-mail, or download questions he's unsure of to Joe. This serves two purposes: It makes the flow of information easier on everyone, and it provides the mental and emotional support the children need.

I feel as if I could go on for months talking about the love Joe and I have for our kids and the little systems we've devised in order to make life easier. Apparently, I'm not alone. I've included two letters in this chapter that poignantly reflect the spirit of parenthood.

The first is from a grandmother who worked hard to achieve her goal of becoming an opera singer. She wrote candidly about her profession, marriage, and children—and the twists and turns of life's journey.

Dear Jennifer,

My dream since childhood was to be an opera singer. My mother told me that I've been singing from the time I was a baby. I sang my way through high school and college, which I attended on a voice scholarship. Chosen to sing leading roles from the age of 17, I also soloed with The Syracuse Symphony on several occasions. Life was very promising in those days.

After marriage, I continued to study and sing with a great teacher at The Metropolitan Opera, and I performed with Met Opera singers. Then came the babies. Raising a family meant being away too often, and relying on nannies and my busy husband. Little by little, I began staying home and turning down singing dates. One day I woke up and found out that it was too late to go back and pick up where I left off. I was mired in suburbia, 25 miles from New York City, in the shadow of the great opera house that I'd hoped to conquer. It was a very painful awakening.

My family means the world to me. But there's still a part of me that will forever be unfulfilled. Watching my children grow and become responsible adults with children of their own has been a joy. My daughter's success as a musician who's very well known in her field has given me great satisfaction. They say we live through our children—there's certainly a lot of me in my daughter. So in a way I've achieved some of my goal through her accomplishments.

— Anna, professional opera singer and music teacher

The second letter I want to share with you is from a news anchor who told me about the emotional experience of leaving her baby and returning to work.

Dear Jennifer,

When my daughter was born, I happily left work for a glorious six-month maternity leave (a true luxury in the working world!). We nuzzled and cuddled and played with her early learning toys. But the day finally came when I had to return to work; consequently, I had to hire someone to look after my little angel.

My husband and I labored over our choice and felt very good about this lovely woman from Poland. Yet when she showed up for a trial day a week before I went back to work, I felt as if I'd throw up. She was sweet and loving, but my husband and I had been the only people who had bathed our baby's downy skin and fed her. I was having a really hard time turning her over. But with a stiff upper lip, I suggested that they go for a walk. After all, I needed to work on my own separation anxiety.

And so, off they went to the park. After they left, I sat down on the couch in my quiet house and cried. It was the beginning of what every working mother knows is a rewarding and painful dichotomy that we live with every day. Next I did what any mom would do—I sneaked around the block to spy on them in the park. They were having a great time. Did I feel better or worse? I'm not sure. But what I did learn over time was that it was not only okay for my daughter to spend time with other grown-ups, it was also good for her. Certainly our most wonderful times are and always have been together as a family, but through our nanny, my daughter developed a love for arts and crafts that I never could have instilled in her. She's also learned about the Polish Christmas tradition and built strong bonds with a woman who, in many ways, has been like a special teacher or camp counselor she'll never forget.

It's never easy to leave your kids and go to work. I'll always feel some strange combination of guilt and pride about this choice, but I've learned to accept that this is what feels right for our family. And as long as we all feel safe and loved, then this home is a great place to be.

— Jessica, television anchorperson

Feeling safe and loved, as Jessica puts it, are two of the most powerful values that we can instill in our children no matter where we are. I wrote about this theme in a speech I recently gave.

Speech to Jack 'n' Jill, Princeton, NJ—2/09/02: "Family: The Fuel We Need"

Good evening, everyone. I've been asked to say a few words about the challenges we face in keeping our families moving in a positive direction, and raising our children while we lead incredibly hectic lives.

It's certainly a hot topic these days. The former First Lady, Hillary Rodham Clinton herself, used the old African proverb "It takes a village to raise a child" as the title and basis for a book. To me, it again underscores how difficult it has become to keep families intact and children in the forefront as our most important resource. In a time like this—time of the modern village—many of us now have the material things that we need, but oftentimes not enough spiritual nourishment or the time we would like to spend with our families. For me, those are the very precious things we can't buy.

But as my parents always said, you truly do make time for the things that are most important to you—the things that will be there in the end. That is *family*. Family will be there after the accolades, awards, and big paychecks end.

It's a bit funny to me sometimes. Working in what I consider one of the most competitive fields out there, I've seen firsthand what people sacrifice to become famous. I sometimes wonder how I've been able to stick to my guns most of the time, saying no to some plum assignments [and] opting instead for the little but . . . forever-treasured moments like hearing my son play his saxophone in the middle-school band. There are the times when my priority was to peek in on my four-year-old son on picture day at preschool.

Don't get me wrong, there have been plenty of years of working weekends; anchoring shows that air live at 4:30 in the morning across the country; and still to this day, there's the typical 12-hour television work day.

But somehow I have managed like so many of you. My husband and I have managed—managed to do what our mothers and fathers did before us. And that is to invest in the futures of our young folks. We tend to think *that* generation, the older generation, had more time. But in retrospect, they didn't.

Many of our parents and their parents before them worked more than one job. In the case of my own mother and father, my father commuted back and forth to Washington, D.C., as the acting deputy administrator of the Drug Enforcement Administration for the United States government. That's while my mother was hands-on with us [her kids], our ballet and music lessons, and our sports and homework. All that while she went back to school to get her college degree.

What is my point? That these *are* tough times for families. But, *nothing*, as I often remind myself, is impossible. Like our parents expected of us, expect excellence from your children. Tell them to strive to be the best. Love your children unequivocally, *even* when the worst happens.

In our house, things have gotten so harried over the years that we've even gone as far implementing our own homework/reward systems, [as] a way to reward our children for a job well-done. My husband devised the plan using charts with smiley faces and various levels offering little treats.

But, parents, when you need help, ask for it. Seek out the help of grandparents, aunts, and uncles who have a particular strength in math or perhaps science.

Believe that there are so many reasons that the efforts you invest in your children will pay off. Look at yourselves and your success. Look at all the things your young people are doing in math and science and in the arts. They are great. Now it's up to us to keep that momentum going.

I never did receive that instruction manual on raising kids. But I've found that my sons have provided the most fun, have taught me the most, and have enriched my life immeasurably—in many ways, they're the very best part of my journey.

CHAPTER FIFTEEN

Bringing
It
Home

I t's a cliché, but there's a lot of truth in the expression, "The more things change, the more they stay the same." I say that because when I look at my life, I realize that in many ways, it's almost a mirror image of my mother's and grandmother's, both of whom married and moved away from home at a fairly young age and raised successful families.

In the beginning of *Life's a Journey—Not a Sprint,* I told you about the admiration I have for my grandmother and how brave she was to travel to the Unites States with a very focused vision for her impending success. But let me explain more about the parallel between us and why I feel encouraged about embarking on the rest of my journey that's yet to come.

As I mentioned before, my grandmother was born in Anguilla, a small island in the British West Indies, in 1898. When she was 24, she came to America—and she entered her 30s during the onset of the Great Depression. She was relatively new to this country but found work as a seamstress and did some housekeeping on the side to make ends meet. My grandfather was a porter and worked at night in a bakery, but he spent as much time as he could with the family.

> *"Never doubt yourself. Many have trials in life. But know that God will direct you on your path."*
> — Bianca O'Neal Richardson, my grandmother

If you look at our lives, my grandmother and I really aren't very different at all (even though I arrived seven decades after her birth). She was known far and wide for having a whole lot of spunk . . . no wonder my mother named me Jennifer *Bianca,* passing down the strong legacy of my grandmother's name and her determination.

When I was growing up, Grandma Bianca and I spent summers together in her home in New York, then time together when she retired back to Anguilla. And we wrote each other dozens and dozens of letters in between those times. "My dearest granddaughter, Jennifer Bianca," she'd say at the start of every note. "I hope this letter finds you well, my dear . . . " Can you imagine being pen pals with your *grandmother?!*

Our bond felt so normal back then—but when I realized that I didn't know too many people who regularly talked with their grandparents about contemporary issues (or even talked to them at all), it struck me how unique my relationship with my grandmother really was.

Now, 14 years after her death, I can see how I'm more like her than I ever knew. You see, Grandma Bianca taught me not to be afraid to go after what I want in life, to know that family is a priority, and to work hard to make my dreams come true. This is now the very same mantra I preach to my own children.

People often think of role models as individuals whom they don't personally know, but my grandmother is mine. More than a half century ago, she believed in pushing the limits when it came to moving beyond racial barriers, economic inequality, and stereotypes associated with gender. She empowered and motivated herself to live beyond the financial means of her parents, and she sought to thrive financially after living through "very modest beginnings." Most of all, her faith and spirit were unwavering, even when food and jobs were scarce during the Depression. She had an amazing amount of dignity and pride regarding her heritage, at a time when African Americans were still fighting for equal rights, and women's suffrage was still in its infancy.

Grandma Bianca continued to push the envelope as she got older by doing things that many considered unprecedented. She became a landlord, acquiring property and homes while making enough money to send back to her native land to help educate and care for others who had yet to see more prosperous economic times. She was a Renaissance woman, thinking outside of the box, setting her own standards and goals, and showing that a woman can accomplish anything.

She was a confident, strong woman with a big heart and loving hands who crocheted ribbons for my hair and sewed my dresses and bedspreads a stitch at a time despite the onset of arthritis. When her daughter (my aunt) died from cancer, Grandma stepped in and raised her kids, even as she still grieved.

This incredible woman was at times weary but never afraid—she'd had one heck of a journey and kept moving forward no matter what was thrown her way. Grandma Bianca was like so many of us today who are trying to do all that we can for our families, going that extra distance in our professions and in our home life to keep our families intact.

Through my grandmother's struggles and her successes, I was shown that it's possible for all of us to live out our dreams and sleep well at night—we can take comfort from the fact that even when things don't work out exactly as planned, we know we've done our best and would do it the same way all over again.

"For every season, there's a reason," Grandma used to tell me. I think what she meant by that is that just as leaves turn colors in the fall and flowers peek through the earth in the spring, life always gives us another chance to start something new.

So, like the seasons, renew your outlook on life with a bold new claim that you can do whatever your heart desires—only *you* should define you. Like the seasons, see an opportunity to change, and venture on a journey that's fresh and exciting. And like the seasons, plan for a ripe harvest of new opportunities but enjoy the moment that you're in.

To all of you who are embarking on a wonderful new journey, I say, "Namaste—the divine in me bows to the divine in you." And I'd like to close this chapter with a few more invaluable words of wisdom from my grandmother: "Live your life child, and live it well."

Thank you, Grandma.

Guiding Your Way
to Life's Successes

I chose to call this book *Life's a Journey—Not a Sprint* for a very deliberate reason. I wanted you to stop and think about where you are and where you're going, and impress upon you that life isn't composed of just one day or one moment—it's an entire collection of experiences that can be enhanced or changed for the better. And I especially wanted women to know that you can set out on the highway of life *at any time,* as long as you have a basic plan that you're willing to cultivate as you go along.

Ask yourself these tough questions: As you travel along life's path, are you simply trying to reach a destination, or are you looking at stretches of road that are filled with opportunities? Know that you're on a long passage, so you needn't become wrapped up in believing that one mistake or misfortune will make or break your life. Again, look beyond the promotions you didn't get or relationships that didn't work out, and remember that you're on a *lifelong* journey. Sometimes that requires you to take a detour—such as making a so-called lateral career move if you're looking to enter a new department, or taking a pay cut to work part time if you need to be with your family more. Sure, it requires hard work to

"We must remember that everything is an experience in life. We'll encounter individuals who help shape us and direct us toward our goals and dreams, but even the people we meet who try to discourage us are gifts in a way and should be valued as such.

"We're on a journey to know about ourselves and others, so we should take our everyday experiences and learn from them. As a student, I view myself as a receptacle of knowledge in the preparatory stages of life.

"There's no way to know exactly when, where, or how we'll be successful. But we always have the choice to prepare ourselves to receive the gifts of our experiences."

— Brianna, graduate student

achieve the goals you've set out for yourself, but understand that the biggest disappointments you'll face will be if you don't seek to live out your dreams at all.

I talked about taking the "slow and steady" road early on in the book, and some people may find that amazing when everything and everybody moves so fast these days. There are certainly times to be aggressive and assertive, but you don't want to constantly speed while you're building your career, your education, or your relationships—for that's when you'll run into roadblocks or crash. Like any good driver, you should take your time so that you can steer clear of trouble whenever possible, and you should make sure that you're armed with a set of tools to solve the problems you simply can't avoid.

I want you to look at yourself, love yourself, and visualize where you want to go. This is something my oldest brother encouraged me to do after he went back to school in his 40s to get his master's degree while working full time. He told me to know who I am on the inside, but visualize myself today as being the person I want to become professionally, academically, or spiritually.

If your goal is to grow spiritually, then start to embody the thoughts, prayers, and deeds that will get you there. If you've always wanted to get a doctorate, see it happening; form a mental image that puts you there already. With commitment and a vision, your success will come. Believe in yourself and know that you can do it.

I can't emphasize enough that I want you to focus on enhancing *all aspects* of your life throughout your passage—your career, your health, and your family and home life. Stop looking at these powerful pieces of your existence as separate parts (for example, one part that can be fed while another is neglected). To be your best you need the harmony of a clear head and a happy heart as well as a plan of action for your future. Conditioning your mind, body, and soul will help keep you focused on the "prize" you're seeking and give you the confidence you need to move forward when times are tough.

And learn to love yourself and value others. In the office, communicate, but be a good listener. At home, be clear about what you need to face the challenges of juggling work, family, and career. Be supportive and loving of one another.

> *"I think that just being yourself and doing positive things that you enjoy is all that it takes to be successful in life. A large part of it comes from having a loving, supportive family and having a job that's fulfilling and meaningful. That's all you need, and the beat will go on."*
> — Sandi, nurse

Finally, always keep in mind that your journey should be cherished and enjoyed. Stop to see the scenery around you along the way. In the Appendix, I've included some affirmations to help you revitalize yourself throughout the year—please use them! And celebrate your successes, no matter how small, for they're the milestones that will let you know that you're heading in the right direction.

Now, just chart your course. You can do it!

APPENDIX

IMPORTANT TOOLS FOR YOUR JOURNEY

52 Weekly Affirmations for Life, Love, Work, and Home

Many people ask me how I find peace in my day when there's so much chaos happening around me. My answer is that I make it a point to read something inspirational before I head out the door each morning. I also spend a few minutes each day quietly thinking of the things I'm thankful for and how

"New beginnings will keep knocking at your door, as if to say, "It's over. Move on—now!" I appreciate the process that we go through in life. Everything is based on the natural and spiritual laws of sowing and reaping. If I sow goodness, peace, love, patience, and joy, I'll receive them in spades (and vice versa). So I look at what I've been blessed to experience—good or bad—in my life and marvel at how I survived those things. I'm thankful for the process: I revel as a caterpillar, I dance while in the cocoon, and I shout for joy as I sprout wings as a butterfly."

— Mia, public relations manager

I plan to tackle the day—even on mornings when my journey feels more like a trek up Mt. Everest than a stroll in the park.

I decided to include the affirmations that I've found to be most helpful so that you can use them to rejuvenate, regenerate, and revitalize areas of your life that need attention. Take time to clean up and clear out whatever you want to change in your life—affirm to yourself that you *can* make those positive changes! Remember that we're blessed with a new day, every day; therefore, we're constantly given the opportunity to live a new way.

Instead of giving you daily affirmations, I've chosen to do it on a weekly and seasonal basis. By doing so, I hope that you'll really take the opportunity to let these positive ideas sprout in your mind as you focus on each one for seven days. Remember—every day holds the promise to build an even better you, so go for it!

• S P R I N G •

Week 1

This week I start my new me with a positive attitude—I am thankful for a fresh start, and I leave negative thoughts of the past behind me. Using a diary, I jot down ten goals I plan to accomplish in the year ahead and why they are important to me.

Week 2

This week I am open to new possibilities in my life that improve both my mind and my body—I meditate for 15 minutes in the morning, then take a daily walk or go to the gym.

Week 3

This week I organize and enhance my workspace—I update computer files and contacts; throw away unnecessary papers; and place a picture, plant, or a small piece of artwork that is special to me on my desk.

Week 4

This week I start to think about my annual review—I write down what I expect to finish this year and what I achieved last year, as well as areas for growth and development.

Week 5

This week I focus on my heart and head. After working all day, I tell my loved ones that they are important and make my life special.

Week 6

This week I send a card of thanks, a handwritten note, or a single flower to someone who helps me through thick and thin.

Week 7

This week I revisit five things that I love about myself—I take five minutes to reflect on them, and I am proud.

Week 8

This week I compliment someone at home on something thoughtful they have done, and someone at work for their outstanding efforts on a particular project.

Week 9

This week I begin to clear out clutter so that I can make use of my time and efforts effectively—I assess what I have and what I do not need.

Week 10

This week I give away what I can no longer use—such as clothing, toys, books, or furniture—to someone who can benefit from them.

Week 11

This week I work on mental cleansing—I rid myself of negative thoughts that overcrowd my mind. I repeat the following each day: "I am a positive individual with a purpose on this earth."

Week 12

This week I take 15 minutes of quiet time to think of nothing but peaceful thoughts—be it amazing scenery or the sounds of the ocean waves—that soothe my soul.

Week 13

This week I begin a phase of reflection for a few minutes each day—I think of moments that have brought me joy, happiness, or fulfillment throughout my life. I relish in the moment.

• S U M M E R •

Week 14

This week I look back with humility on what has made me the individual I am today. I acknowledge the power of my progress, appreciate how far I have come in my life, and feel good about how I have turned negative situations into positive ones.

Week 15

This week I think of five reasons why I am proud of myself in my professional life—I say, "Job well done," for coming up with a new idea or saving a project that was in jeopardy.

Week 16

This week I find five reasons why I am proud of myself in my personal life (for example: "I am proud to be a class mom, mentor, Girl Scout leader, book-club member, and singer in the church choir").

Week 17

This week I take the time to smell the flowers, literally—I arrange some flowers around my home or in the entryway of my apartment; and I put a fresh, fragrant arrangement on my desk to enjoy throughout the week.

Week 18

This week *I* am the blossom—I spray myself with my favorite colognes or perfumes in the mornings to awaken my senses, trying a different one each day.

Week 19

This week I sprinkle some scented powder to my sheets before bed, or put some fresh rose petals on my nightstand.

Week 20

This week I add candles to my aromatherapy experience—I light a sweet-smelling citrus or woodsy candle while I eat dinner or take a shower.

Week 21

This week I enjoy the great outdoors—I rise a few minutes early to sit on my front steps or back porch to enjoy my morning coffee before leaving for work or getting the kids ready for school.

Week 22

This week I plan to have lunch with a co-worker or friend— I get away from my desk and go to a café or sandwich shop to break up my day.

Week 23

This week I walk to get the morning paper and my favorite beverage rather than drive—I use the exercise as a pick-me-up in the morning.

Week 24

This week I do one fun outdoor activity, such as riding my bike on a Saturday morning, putting on my headphones and walking around the block, or taking my indoor exercise routine outside by running up some steps or jumping rope in the park.

Week 25

This week I am conscious of the role that social interaction plays in my life at home and at work—I take a few extra minutes to say good morning to those around me or ask how their day is going.

Week 26

This week I call, or send a card to, a loved one whom I have not contacted in a while.

· F A L L ·

Week 27

This week I head to a matinee with a friend, rent a video, or share some popcorn on a Friday night with the family to make the evening special.

Week 28

This week I take a day to surprise my co-workers by buying the morning coffee and bagels or passing out cookies as an afternoon treat.

Week 29

This week I think about the importance of balancing work and rest—if it has been a while since I have taken a vacation, I plan one now.

Week 30

This week I use one weekend day to catch up on much-needed rest—I ask my spouse or family member to help out with the kids.

Week 31

This week I plan an overnight getaway—perhaps I leave work early on Friday afternoon for an overnight stay at a bed-and-breakfast retreat that is a short drive away.

Week 32

This week I keep the cooking simple—I order take-out, or make something easy in the slow cooker.

Week 33

This week I begin a regimen of better financial fitness— I make out a budget, pay attention to where money is being wasted, and determine where I can maximize savings.

Week 34

This week I work on clearing up old bills, credit problems, or debt that has been hanging over my head. I seek out a reputable financial advisor to review my long-term strategies, from IRAs to 401(k) saving plans.

Week 35

This week I review my credit-card statements—I make steps toward paying off balances and reducing my interest rate.

Week 36

This week I bring my lunch to work rather than eating out to see how much money I have saved at the end of the week.

Week 37

This week I refocus and forge ahead with the projects and goals I laid out at the beginning of the year—I cross off the goals I have accomplished and highlight those that remain.

Week 38

This week I do at least one thing that helps me achieve the goals I have yet to accomplish.

Week 39

This week I attach the words *You can do it!* to my mirror.

• W I N T E R •

Week 40

This week I treat myself to something special to reward myself for the achievements I have made thus far.

Week 41

This week I take comfort in knowing that I am loved, which includes loving myself—I treat myself and others with kindness and compassion.

Week 42

This week I make my surroundings more comfortable—perhaps I buy a soft throw or fluffy pillow to lie on.

Week 43

This week, I do something special just for me—I soak my feet, get a manicure, or have some fresh fruit and sparkling cider before the family rises.

Week 44

This week, I spice up an old favorite—I add a few marshmallows to my hot chocolate or drizzle my coffee with caramel before I head to work or school.

Week 45

This week I kick off a period of thanks and gratitude—I write down ten things that I am thankful for.

Week 46

This week I tell those I am thankful for why I am glad they came into my life.

Week 47

This week I frame a picture of someone who has made a difference in my life and put it on my desk at work or in my home office.

Week 48

This week I show my children old photos of their grandparents or aunts and uncles—I share with them what makes our family special.

Week 49

This week I read a poem, verse, scripture, or saying that inspires me each morning.

Week 50

This week I search for a new level of inspiration at work and at home—I think about what drives me and how I can turn that energy into new and meaningful opportunities.

Week 51

This week I praise those around me at work, home, or school for all they have done to help me through a busy year.

Week 52

This week I look at myself in the mirror and say with a sense of pride, "I am uplifted for the strides I have made this year and am looking forward to peace, prosperity, and progress in the next year."

"Becoming more confident on the job is an ongoing task. The key is to learn everything about your career from past to present. By increasing your knowledge, you'll naturally increase confidence about your trade. In addition, learn from the veterans. Their knowledge and experience is valuable and will be worth more than anything you can get from a textbook."
— Amanda, stock trader

I hope these positive, uplifting ideas will put a little spring in your step all throughout the year!

14 Nutritious
and
Delicious Recipes

A s I mentioned in Chapter 10, living healthfully will optimize your journey, for when you feel better, you'll act better. You will be able to perform at your maximum potential.

But after working all day, who has time to cook, let alone make fresh, creative meals? Not to mention the fact that each family member has their own preferences: for example, my husband likes meats; I'm a lover of vegetables; one of our sons eats everything; the other, next to nothing. So it's hard to get a meal going that everyone can enjoy, is healthy, and is easy on the chef.

> *"The key to changing bad eating habits comes from learning how to accept yourself and your body exactly as it is. When I claimed myself as beautiful (with 50 extra pounds on my body) and I felt in my core that I was loved and valued—that's when I finally found my way into healthy eating and exercising."*
>
> — Rebecca, religious writer

Here, I've included 14 recipes that I know from experience will make life a little less complicated. They come from the National Institutes of Health (NIH) and are just a small sampling of the agency's "Stay Young at Heart" recipes. What I've chosen for you comes from the four broad categories of chicken, fish, beef, and vegetarian entrees.

If you're like me, you know that food preparation—from grocery shopping to getting dinner on the table—-takes a lot of time and effort. However, if you're organized, you can spend as little or as much time as you'd like in the kitchen. In my house, my husband does most of the cooking. With my busy job and his travel schedule, we've come up with a few other ideas to keep the household running smoothly where the meals are concerned.

Jennifer and Joe's Tips for Meals

We plan our family meals on a weekly basis. That means that we usually know what we're going to have a week ahead of time. It doesn't get boring, because we include fun meals that we like to name. For example, we'll have Mile-High Nachos, Jennifer's Baby-Back Ribs, or Joe's Thursday Night Special (which is a grilled dish). Then we just make a simple handwritten menu that lists each day's fare, Monday through Thursday. Friday and Saturday nights are open to pizza or burgers or whatever our hearts desire (and our stomachs can handle).

On Sundays, we prepare what we can in advance. So if there's meat to marinate or vegetables to chop, it's out of the way. We came up with this system by trial and error, since we're big on cooking fresh foods but struggled with getting home in the evenings and trying to cook everything from scratch.

In addition, if we have the recipes, we can simply take that information to the grocery store, get all the ingredients at one time, and pick up a salad and side dish as well.

Now, on to the recipes, which are specifically from the NIH's National Heart, Lung, and Blood Institute. (You'll notice that a number of these dishes I included use garlic, basil, oregano, and fresh lemon, which are ingredients that will please the palate and excite your aromatic senses.) *Bon appetit!*

Chicken and Turkey Dishes

20-Minute Chicken Creole

This quick Southern dish contains no added fat and very little added salt in its spicy tomato sauce.

Ingredients:
Nonstick spray, as needed
4 medium chicken-breast halves, skinned, boned, and
    cut into 1-inch strips*
1 can (14 oz.) tomatoes, cut up**
1 cup low-sodium chili sauce
1½ cups green peppers, chopped (1 large)
½ cup celery, chopped
¼ cup onion, chopped
2 cloves minced garlic
1 Tbsp. fresh or 1 tsp. dried basil
1 Tbsp. fresh or 1 tsp. dried parsley
½ tsp. crushed red pepper
½ tsp. salt

Directions:
Spray a deep skillet with nonstick spray coating. Preheat pan over high heat.

Cook chicken in hot skillet, stirring, for 3 to 5 minutes, or until no longer pink. Reduce heat. Add the rest of the ingredients. Bring to a boil; reduce heat and simmer, covered, for 10 minutes.

Serve over hot cooked rice or whole-wheat pasta.

You can substitute 1 lb. boneless, skinless, chicken breast, cut into 1-inch strips.
**To cut back on sodium, try low-sodium canned tomatoes.*
Yield: 4 servings
Serving size: 1½ cups
Each serving provides: Calories: 255; Total fat: 3 g; Saturated fat: less than 1 g; Cholesterol: 100 mg; Sodium: 465 mg

Spaghetti with Turkey Meat Sauce

Using nonstick cooking spray, ground turkey, and no added salt helps make this classic dish heart-healthy.

Ingredients:
    Nonstick cooking spray, as needed
    1 lb. ground turkey
    1 can (28 oz.) tomatoes, cut up
    1 cup finely chopped green pepper
    1 cup finely chopped onion
    2 cloves garlic, minced
    1 tsp. dried oregano, crushed
    1 tsp. black pepper
    1 lb. spaghetti, uncooked

Directions:

Spray a large skillet with nonstick cooking spray. Preheat over high heat. Add turkey; cook, stirring occasionally, for 5 minutes. Drain fat and discard.

Stir in tomatoes with their juice; add green pepper, onion, garlic, oregano, and black pepper. Bring to a boil; reduce heat. Simmer covered for 15 minutes, stirring occasionally. Remove cover; simmer for 15 minutes more. (If you like a creamier sauce, give sauce a whirl in your blender or food processor.) Meanwhile, cook spaghetti in unsalted water.

Drain well.

Serve sauce over spaghetti.

Yield: 6 servings
Serving size: 5 oz. sauce and 9 oz. spaghetti
Each serving provides: Calories: 330; Total fat: 5 g; Saturated fat: 1 g; Cholesterol: 60 mg; Sodium: 280 mg

❧❀❧

Very Lemony Chicken

Using skinless chicken breasts means this tangy dish is low in saturated fat and cholesterol.

Ingredients:

1½ lbs. chicken breast, skin and fat removed
½ cup fresh lemon juice
2 Tbsp. white-wine vinegar
½ cup fresh sliced lemon peel
3 tsp. chopped fresh oregano or 1 tsp dried oregano, crushed

1 medium onion, sliced
¼ tsp. salt
Black pepper, to taste
½ tsp. paprika

Directions:

Place chicken in 13″ x 9″ x 2″ glass baking dish. Mix lemon juice, vinegar, lemon peel, oregano, and onions—pour over chicken. Cover and marinate in refrigerator several hours or overnight, turning occasionally. Sprinkle with salt, pepper, and paprika.

Cover and bake at 325° F for 30 minutes. Uncover and bake 30 minutes more or until done.

Yield: 4 servings
Serving size: One chicken breast with sauce
Each serving provides: Calories: 154; Total fat: 5 g; Saturated fat: 2 g; Cholesterol: 63 mg; Sodium: 202 mg

Fish Dishes

Spinach-Stuffed Sole

A scant amount of oil and part-skim mozzarella cheese gives this lower-fat dish a Mediterranean flavor.

Ingredients:

Nonstick cooking spray, as needed
1 tsp. olive oil
½ lb. fresh mushrooms, sliced
½ lb. fresh spinach, chopped

¼ tsp. oregano leaves, crushed
1 clove garlic, minced
1½ lbs. sole fillets or other white fish
2 Tbsp. sherry
4 oz. part-skim mozzarella cheese, grated

Directions:

Preheat oven to 400°F. Spray a 10″ x 6″ baking dish with non-stick cooking spray.

Heat oil in skillet; sauté mushrooms about 3 minutes or until tender. Add spinach, and continue cooking about 1 minute or until spinach is barely wilted. Remove from heat; drain liquid into prepared baking dish. Add oregano and garlic to drained sautéed vegetables; stir to mix ingredients.

Divide vegetable mixture evenly among fillets, placing filling in center of each fillet. Roll fillet around mixture, and place seam-side down in prepared baking dish.

Sprinkle with sherry, then grated mozzarella cheese. Bake 15 to 20 minutes or until fish flakes easily. Lift out with a slotted spoon.

Yield: 4 servings
Serving size: 1 fillet roll
Each serving provides: Calories: 262; Total fat: 8 g; Saturated fat: 4 g; Cholesterol: 95 mg; Sodium: 312 mg

❧❧❧

Spicy Baked Fish

Ingredients:

Nonstick cooking spray, as needed
1 lb. cod (or other fish) fillet
1 Tbsp. olive oil
1 tsp. spicy seasoning, salt free

Directions:

Preheat oven to 350°F. Coat a casserole dish with cooking-oil spray. Wash and dry fish, place in dish. Mix oil and seasoning, and drizzle over fish.

Bake uncovered for 15 minutes or until fish flakes with fork. Cut into 4 pieces. Serve with rice.

Yield: 4 servings
Serving size: 1 piece (3 oz.)
Each serving provides: Calories 133; Fat: 1 g; Saturated fat: 0 g; Cholesterol: 77 mg; Sodium: 119 mg

❧

Fish Veronique

Defatted chicken broth and low-fat milk lower the fat content, yet give the sauce a rich, creamy taste.

Ingredients:

Nonstick cooking spray, as needed
1 lb. white fish (cod, sole, turbot, etc.)
¼ tsp. salt

⅛ tsp. black pepper

¼ cup dry white wine

¼ cup chicken stock or broth (skim fat from top)

1 Tbsp. lemon juice

1 Tbsp. soft margarine

2 Tbsp. flour

¾ cup low-fat (1 percent) or skim milk

½ cup seedless grapes

Directions:

Spray 10˝ x 6˝ baking dish with nonstick spray. Place fish in pan, and sprinkle with salt and pepper.

Mix wine, stock, and lemon juice in small bowl and pour over fish. Cover and bake at 350°F for 15 minutes.

Melt margarine in small saucepan. Remove from heat and blend in flour. Gradually add milk, and cook over moderately low heat, stirring constantly until thickened.

Remove fish from oven, and pour liquid from baking dish into cream sauce, stirring until blended. Pour sauce over fish and sprinkle with grapes.

Broil about 4 inches from heat 5 minutes or until sauce starts to brown.

Yield: 4 servings

Serving size: 1 fillet with sauce

Each serving provides: Total fat: 4 g; Saturated fat: 1 g; Cholesterol: 53 mg; Sodium: 316 mg

Vegetarian Dishes

Zucchini Lasagna

Ingredients:
Nonstick cooking spray, as needed
½ lb. cooked lasagna noodles, (in unsalted water)
¾ cup mozzarella cheese, part-skim, grated
1½ cups cottage cheese, fat free
¼ cup Parmesan cheese, grated
1½ cups zucchini, raw, sliced
2½ cups tomato sauce, no salt added
2 tsp. dried basil
2 tsp. dried oregano
¼ cup onion, chopped
1 clove garlic
⅛ tsp. black pepper

Directions:
Preheat oven to 350°F. Lightly coat a 9″ x 13″ baking dish with cooking spray. In a small bowl, combine ⅛ cup mozzarella and 1 Tbsp. Parmesan cheese. Set aside. In a medium bowl, combine remaining mozzarella and Parmesan cheese with all the cottage cheese. Mix well and set aside.

Combine tomato sauce with remaining ingredients. Spread a thin layer of tomato sauce in the bottom of the baking dish. Add a third of the noodles in a single layer. Spread half of the cottage cheese mixture on top. Add a layer of zucchini. Repeat layering. Add a thin coating of sauce. Top with noodles, sauce, and reserved cheese mixture. Cover with aluminum foil.

Bake 30 to 40 minutes. Cool for 10 to 15 minutes. Cut into 6 portions.

Yield: 6 servings
Serving size: 1 piece
Each serving provides: Calories: 276; Total Fat: 5 g; Saturated fat: 2 g; Cholesterol: 11 mg; Sodium: 380 mg

✄⊱✄

Summer Vegetable Spaghetti

This lively vegetarian pasta dish contains no added fat or oil, is low in cholesterol, and is good hot or cold.

Ingredients:
2 cups small yellow onions, cut in eighths
2 cups chopped, peeled, fresh, ripe tomatoes (about 1 lb.)
2 cups thinly sliced yellow and green squash (about 1 lb.)
1½ cups cut fresh green beans (about ½ lb.)
⅔ cup water
2 Tbsp. minced fresh parsley
1 clove garlic, minced
½ tsp. chili powder
½ tsp. salt
Black pepper, to taste
1 can (6 oz.) tomato paste
1 lb. uncooked spaghetti
½ cup grated Parmesan cheese

Directions:
Combine first 10 ingredients in large saucepan; cook for 10 minutes, then stir in tomato paste. Cover and cook gently for 15 minutes, stirring occasionally until vegetables are tender.

Cook spaghetti in unsalted water according to package directions.

Spoon sauce over drained hot spaghetti, and sprinkle Parmesan cheese over top.

Yield: 9 servings
Serving size: 1 cup spaghetti and ¾ cup sauce with vegetables
Each serving provides: Calories: 279; Total fat: 3 g; Saturated fat: 1 g; Cholesterol: 4 mg; Sodium: 173 mg

ↄ⊱⊰ↄ

Classic Macaroni and Cheese

Low-fat cheese and skim milk help make this favorite dish heart-healthy.

Ingredients:
2 cups macaroni
½ cup chopped onion
½ cup evaporated skim milk
1 medium egg, beaten
¼ tsp. black pepper
1¼ cups sharp cheddar cheese (4 oz.), finely shredded, low fat
Nonstick cooking spray

Directions:
Cook macaroni according to directions. (Do not add salt to the cooking water.) Drain and set aside.

Coat a casserole dish with nonstick cooking spray. Preheat oven to 350°F. Lightly spray saucepan with nonstick cooking spray.

Add onions to saucepan and sauté for about 3 minutes. In another bowl, combine macaroni, onions, and the remaining ingredients; mix thoroughly. Transfer mixture into casserole dish

Bake for 25 minutes or until bubbly. Let stand for 10 minutes before serving.

Yield: 8 servings
Serving size: ½ cup
Each serving provides: Calories: 200; Fat: 4 g; Saturated fat: 2 g; Cholesterol: 34 mg; Sodium: 120 mg

༺࿐༻

Black Beans with Rice

A delicious Caribbean favorite that's cholesterol free and made with very little added fat.

Ingredients:
1 lb. dry black beans
7 cups water
1 medium green pepper, coarsely chopped
1½ cups chopped onion
1 Tbsp. vegetable oil
2 bay leaves
1 clove garlic, minced
½ tsp. salt
1 Tbsp. vinegar (or lemon juice)
6 cups rice, cooked in unsalted water
1 jar (4 oz.) sliced pimento, drained
1 lemon, cut into wedges

Directions:
Soak beans overnight in cold water. Drain and rinse.

In large soup pot or Dutch oven, stir together beans, water, green pepper, onion, oil, bay leaves, garlic, and salt. Cover and boil 1 hour. Reduce heat and simmer, covered, 3 to 4 hours or until beans are very tender. Stir occasionally, and add water if needed. Remove about ⅓ of the beans, mash; and return to pot. Stir and heat through. Remove bay leaves, and stir in vinegar or lemon juice when ready to serve.

Serve over rice. Garnish with sliced pimento and lemon wedges.

Yield: 6 servings
Serving size: 8 oz
Each serving provides: Calories: 561; Total fat: 4 g; Saturated fat: 1 g; Cholesterol: 0 mg; Sodium: 193 mg

ॐ·ॐ·ॐ

Caribbean Pink Beans

Ingredients:
1 lb. pink beans
10 cups water
2 medium plantains, finely chopped
1 large tomato, finely chopped
1 small red pepper, finely chopped
1 medium white onion, finely chopped
3 cloves garlic, finely chopped
1½ tsp. salt

Directions:
Rinse beans and put them in a large pot with 10 cups of water. Place the pot in the refrigerator and allow beans to soak overnight.

Cook the beans until they're soft. Add more water as needed while the beans are cooking. Add the plantains, tomato, pepper, onion, garlic, and salt. Continue cooking at low heat until the plantains are soft.

Option: Serve with rice.
Yield: 16 servings
Serving size: ½ cup
Each serving provides: Calories: 133; Total fat: Less than 1 g; Saturated fat: Less than 1 g; Cholesterol: 0 mg; Sodium: 205 mg

❧

Black Skillet Beef with Greens and Red Potatoes

A heart-healthy, one-dish meal that's made with lean top round beef, lots of vegetables, and a spicy herb mixture.

Ingredients:
1 lb. top ground beef
1 Tbsp. paprika
1½ tsp. oregano
½ tsp. chili powder
¼ tsp. garlic powder
¼ tsp. black pepper
⅛ tsp. red pepper
⅛ tsp. dry mustard
8 red-skinned potatoes, halved
3 cups finely chopped onion
2 cups beef broth
2 large garlic cloves, minced
2 large carrots, peeled, cut into very thin 2½-inch strips
2 bunches (½-lb. each) mustard greens, kale, or turnip greens, stems removed, coarsely torn
Nonstick spray coating, as needed

Directions:

Partially freeze beef. Thinly slice across the grain into long strips ⅛-inch thick and 3 inches wide.

Combine paprika, oregano, chili powder, garlic powder, black pepper, red pepper, and dry mustard. Coat strips of meat with the spice mixture.

Coat a large heavy skillet with nonstick spray coating. Preheat pan over high heat. Add meat; cook, stirring for 5 minutes. Add potatoes, onion, broth, and garlic. Cook covered, over medium heat for 20 minutes. Stir in carrots; lay greens over top; and cook, covered, until carrots are tender, about 15 minutes.

Serve in large serving bowl, with crusty bread for dunking.

Yield: 6 servings
Serving size: 7 oz.
Each serving provides: Calories: 342; Total fat: 4 g; Saturated fat: 1 g; Cholesterol: 45 mg; Sodium: 101 mg

❧

Scrumptious Meat Loaf

Use extra-lean ground beef to lower the fat content in this meat loaf.

Ingredients:

1 lb. ground beef, extra lean
½ cup tomato paste (4 oz.)
¼ cup onion, chopped
¼ cup green peppers
¼ cup red peppers

1 cup fresh tomatoes, blanched and chopped
½ tsp. mustard, low sodium
¼ tsp. ground black pepper
½ tsp. hot pepper, chopped
2 cloves garlic, chopped
2 stalks scallion, chopped
½ tsp. ginger, ground
⅛ tsp. nutmeg, ground
1 tsp. orange rind, grated
½ tsp. thyme, crushed
¼ cup bread crumbs, finely grated

Directions:

Mix all ingredients together. Place in 1-pound loaf pan (preferably a pan with a drip rack), and bake covered at 350° F for 50 minutes.

Uncover pan and continue baking for 12 minutes.

Yield: 6 servings
Serving size: 6 (1¼-inch-thick slices)
Each serving provides: Calories: 193; Fat: 9 g; Saturated fat: 3 g

Stir-Fried Beef and Potatoes

Ingredients:

1½ lbs. sirloin steak
2 tsp. vegetable oil
1 clove garlic, minced
1 tsp. vinegar
⅛ tsp. salt

⅛ tsp. pepper
2 large onions, sliced
1 large tomato, sliced
3 cups boiled potatoes, diced

Directions:

Trim fat from steak and cut into small, thin pieces. In a large skillet, heat oil, and sauté garlic until garlic is golden. Add steak, vinegar, salt, and pepper. Cook for 6 minutes, stirring beef until brown. Add onion and tomato. Cook until onion is transparent.

Serve with boiled potatoes and white rice.

Yield: 6 servings
Serving size: 1¼ cups
Each serving with potatoes and rice provides: Calories: 549; Total fat: 8 g; Saturated fat: 2 g; Cholesterol: 56 mg; Sodium: 288 mg

> *"I give a lot of energy to self-care. I have a therapist; I get massages; I lift weights with a personal trainer; I work out almost daily; I'm careful about what I eat; and I make time to feed my spiritual life through friendships and prayer. What I have found is that this attention to myself (something I would have thought selfish as a child) frees me for service in the world in ways I never could have imagined."*
> — Mary Lynne, researcher

ENDNOTES

Chapter 5:

1. This quote taken from *Quotations from Booker T. Washington* compiled by E. Davidson Washington, Tuskegee Institute Press, 1938.

Chapter 10:

1. Centers for Disease Control and Prevention. National Center for Health Statistics. *Prevalence of Overweight and Obesity Among Adults: United States, 1999–2000.*

2. Centers for Disease Control and Prevention. National Center for Chronic Disease Prevention and Health Promotion—Nutrition & Physical Activity.

From women's issues to Wall Street, **Jennifer Lewis-Hall** is a veteran reporter, Emmy-nominated journalist, and sought-after public speaker whose career in television, newspapers, and magazines has spanned nearly two decades. She's been seen around the world throughout CNBC's *Business Day,* and has also graced the network airways on NBC's *Early Today.* In addition, she has occasionally anchored *The Wall Street Journal Report.*

Lewis-Hall is a wife and mother who's received numerous awards for her professional accomplishments as well as civic contributions. She's one of the youngest women ever to be inducted into the Douglass Society at Douglass College for outstanding achievement, and she's shared her insights on raising children, breaking into the workplace, and achieving success in business with numerous organizations.

❧❧❧

We hope you enjoyed this Hay House book.
If you would like to receive a free catalog featuring additional
Hay House books and products, or if you would like information
about the Hay Foundation, please contact:

Hay House, Inc.
P.O. Box 5100
Carlsbad, CA 92018-5100

(760) 431-7695 or (800) 654-5126
(760) 431-6948 (fax) or (800) 650-5115 (fax)
www.hayhouse.com

❧❧❧

Published and distributed in Australia by:
Hay House Australia Pty Ltd, 18/36 Ralph St., Alexandria
NSW 2015 • *Phone:* 612-9669-4299 • *Fax:* 612-9669-4144 •
E-mail: info@hayhouse.com.au

Published and Distributed in the United Kingdom by:
Hay House UK, Ltd. • Unit 202, Canalot Studios •
222 Kensal Rd., London W10 5BN • *Phone:* 020-8962-1230 •
Fax: 020-8962-1239

Distributed in Canada by: Raincoast • 9050 Shaughnessy St.,
Vancouver, B.C. V6P 6E5 •
Phone: (604) 323-7100 • *Fax:* (604) 323-2600

❧❧❧